# The Business of Hotels

By the same author

*Britain – Workshop or Service Centre to the World?*
*The British Hotel and Catering Industry*
*Dictionary of Travel, Tourism and Hospitality*
*Europeans on Holiday*
*Higher Education and Research in Tourism in Western Europe*
*Historical Development of Tourism* (with A. J. Burkart)
*Holiday Surveys Examined*
*The Management of Tourism* (with A. J. Burkart eds)
*Managing Tourism* (ed.)
*A Manual of Hotel Reception* (with J. R. S. Beavis)
*Paying Guests*
*Profile of the Hotel and Catering Industry* (with D. W. Airey)
*Tourism and Productivity*
*Tourism Council of the South Pacific Corporate Plan*
*Tourism Employment in Wales*
*Tourism: Past, Present and Future* (with A. J. Burkart)
*Trends in Tourism: World Experience and England's Prospects*
*Trends in World Tourism*
*Your Manpower* (with J. Denton)

# The Business of Hotels

S. Medlik

Third Edition

BUTTERWORTH
HEINEMANN

Butterworth-Heinemann Ltd
Linacre House, Jordan Hill, Oxford OX2 8DP

℞ A member of the Reed Elsevier plc group

OXFORD   LONDON   BOSTON
MUNICH   NEW DELHI   SINGAPORE   SYDNEY
TOKYO   TORONTO   WELLINGTON

First published 1980
Reprinted 1985, 1986, 1987 (twice)
Second edition 1989
Reprinted 1990, 1991, 1993
Third edition 1994
Reprinted 1995

© S. Medlik 1980, 1989, 1994

**British Library Cataloguing in Publication Data**
Medlik, S.
    Business of Hotels – 3Rev.ed
    I. Title
    647.94068

ISBN 0 7506 2080 3

Typeset by Deltatype Ltd, Ellesmere Port, Cheshire
Printed and Bound in Great Britain by
Hartnolls Limited, Bodmin, Cornwall.

# Contents

PART 1  BASIC HOTEL CONCEPTS

# Tables

# Figures

# Preface

In business and management literature some authors have approached their subject through the study of work, notably Frederick Winslow Taylor and the Gilbreths. Others, for example, Henri Fayol and Peter Drucker, did so through the analysis of managerial experience. The third and most recent influence has been writers such as Frederick Herzberg and Douglas McGregor who brought knowledge to bear from behavioural sciences on management thought. There are few examples of these three schools in the literature of hotel management.

Hotels have been seen by most as a rather specialized type of business. They attracted many successful entrepreneurs and managers, but both have been too busy making a success of their hotels to write about them. The academics and consultants concerned with hotels rarely took on the task of explaining the hotel business to a wider public other than lecturing about it, articles in the press or in reports for their clients.

The large and growing volume of books on hotels appears to have taken several distinct directions. There are books devoted to the skills and techniques of particular hotel activities such as hotel reception, housekeeping, food and drink service and especially food preparation. Others are concerned with accounting, marketing, personnel management, maintenance and other specialist functions of the hotel. There are also several economic and historical studies of the industry. Most of these and the few dealing more or less comprehensively with the hotel as a whole almost invariably embrace catering activities outside hotels, rather than concentrating on hotels. Indeed few books on hotel management have been published anywhere since Lucius Boomer's classic *Hotel*

*Management*\* first appeared more than fifty years ago. In the same period only limited progress has been made in the translation of business and management theory from manufacturing to service industries generally and to hotels in particular. This is particularly striking in view of the growth of hotels and of education and training for hotel management in the intervening decades.

An hotel is a business with its own products and markets, technology and methods, which does not lend itself to easy analysis. It offers several distinct products in varying combinations for sale to many markets. It combines production and sale under one roof. It is in close and intimate contact with its customers who consume hotel products at the point of sale. It has a high capital to sales ratio, yet it tends to be labour intensive. Therefore, in many respects a meaningful treatment of hotel activity calls for recognition and explanation of these and other realities, rather than an adaptation of general theories to the hotel business.

This book has no ambitions to replace general business and management reading for the hotelier nor to include between two covers all that enters into the business of hotelkeeping. It is an attempt to fill a gap felt for some time by students, teachers and practitioners, for a book describing the hotel as a business. In this the approach has been to provide a simple and reasonably comprehensive outline rather than a detailed treatment of some or all aspects of the hotel business in depth. Suggestions for further reading on particular aspects are made for each of the fifteen chapters of the book; material used in writing it and other relevant literature is listed in the bibliography.

The supporting reading suggested for use as an extension of this book and the bibliography are confined to one hundred sources, in the main to those available as separate publications and, with few exceptions, published in Britain. Much more reading material related to each chapter of the book is available in the form of articles in journals, papers presented at conferences, and in what has been published otherwise in one form or another both in Britain and elsewhere. It is suggested that teachers are in the best position to produce their own collateral reading lists with the desired focus and emphasis for their own courses and students. Likewise, those in other countries can decide whether to draw on

---

\* Boomer, L., (1925) *Hotel Management – Principles and Practice*, Harper & Brothers, New York and London. In this author's view subsequent revised editions in 1931 and 1938 did not match what the President of Hotel Waldorf-Astoria Corporation, New York, wrote himself in the first edition.

the suggested further reading and bibliography included in this book, or to substitute material known to them, or perhaps adopt a combination of the two approaches.

For the student and the teacher of hotel management the whole book and each of its chapters is, therefore, intended to provide a framework, within which the hotel business may be examined in such depth as may be required by particular courses, with or without the use of other supporting material. For the practitioner – the owner, director or manager – the book may help to organize and formalize what they may have learnt in a less systematic way by experience and also perhaps contribute to a more balanced view of their businesss. Newcomers to the hotel business and others with a professional interest in understanding it should find the book a suitable introduction to its working.

The specialist reader will soon note that often only one chapter is devoted to his or her own field, for example, to marketing, finance and accounts, and to staffing, although on closer examination it becomes apparent that neither these three topics nor others are confined to particular chapters. In fact, if any aspects tend to dominate the text, they are markets, money and people, in the belief that hotels have to pay particular attention to them in order to ensure sustained viability, within the total framework of their operations.

Most readers will discover what will seem to them important omissions. Legal considerations, which increasingly affect the hotel business, are largely omitted, because they differ from one country to another and because they are adequately documented elsewhere. Technical considerations receive scant attention for similar reasons, and because their applicability also varies greatly according to the size and type of business, for meaningful treatment here. Other aspects, of significance only to a small minority of hotel operations, are also neglected.

Many people have influenced the writing of this book and its contents, and sometimes that influence goes back for many years. The first was John Fuller, then Head of Department at Battersea Polytechnic, who was responsible for my entry into the hotel business, for making it possible for me to get to know it, and to become fascinated by it in the 1950s. The second was A. H. Jones of Grosvenor House, who directed that hotel for nearly thirty years, the last ten of which coincided with the first ten years of my professional involvement with hotels, and who was among the first in Britain to typify the role of an hotelman as a businessman and a leader in his industry. The third was Dean Howard B. Meek, founder of the Cornell University School of Hotel Administration, who had a greater impact on future generations of hotelmen than most, and in the process also on hotel management education and training. The fourth was Lord Crowther, who as chairman of Trust Houses brought his many skills to bear on a large corporate hotel organization and on its role in the industry and in the economy in the 1960s and early 1970s. Last but not least, I am indebted to Dr D. M. A. Leggett, first Vice-Chancellor of the University of Surrey, who made it possible, through his help and encouragement, for hotel management studies to become established in a university.

In my day-to-day work I benefited a great deal from discussions and sometimes joint authorship with several of my colleagues at the University of Surrey: John Beavis in hotel reception, as is evident from Chapter 4; John Burkart and Victor Middleton in marketing, and this shaped Chapters 1, 2 and 10; Roger Doswell in hotel planning and this is reflected in Chapters 2 and 10; Philip Nailon in several directions, with a bearing on Chapters 3, 7 and 8.

Three lesser-known books influenced this one in particular: G. Campbell-Smith's *Marketing of the Meal Experience*,* through its translation of the marketing concept; D. A. Fearn's *The Practice of General Management – Catering Applications*†, through some of the thoughts on management expressed in it; and L. S. Fenton's and N. A. Fowler's and their contributors' *Hotel Accounts and their Audit*††, through the ideas it provided on the approach and structure of this book.

Several people read through drafts of chapters and commented on them, in particular Michael Nightingale (Chapters 1-6), and Geoff Parkinson (Chapters 9 and 12), as well as others who prefer not to be named.

As an author I cannot claim that any of those mentioned would agree completely with what appears in these pages, and wish to stress that any shortcomings in this volume are entirely my own. But I remain very much indebted to all whose influence I have acknowledged and also to others whose contribution may have gone unrecorded.

*Guildford 1978*                                                    *S. Medlik*

---

* University of Surrey, 1967.
† Macdonald, 1971.
†† The Institute of Chartered Accountants in England and Wales, 1978.

# Preface to the Third Edition

The first edition of this book was written in the late 1970s. Since it was published in 1980, it has gone into a second edition and has been reprinted a number of times. Before I embarked on the preparation of the third edition, the publishers sent a copy of the book with a questionnaire to lecturers known to use the book in their teaching and to a similar number of 'non-users', seeking their comments on it.

What more than one respondent liked most about the book was its format and structure, conciseness and clear presentation; the content, wide scope and international dimensions; the wealth of statistics and the suggestions for further reading.

Multiple suggestions for a new edition included still more (updated) statistics; more examples and information about hotel companies and the hotel industry; more graphical illustrations.

The third edition owes much to the views expressed in this survey. A major aim has been to show the hotel business in the 1990s rather than the 1970s and 1980s as portrayed in earlier editions, and most statistics refer to the early 1990s. All but a few of the forty tables of the last edition have been replaced by some fifty new ones and these include for the first time data on hotel operations in a number of European countries. Twenty charts and diagrams and thirty shaded entries highlight significant data, concepts and comparisons, quotes and extracts from various sources. The main text is also supplemented by ten appendices.

Suggestions for further reading for each chapter and the list of books for students and professionals are again confined to 100 sources mainly published in the United Kingdom, but have been completely revised to reflect a major output of new titles since this book was first published; with only a few exceptions, the list includes books published between 1980 and 1993; most earlier texts that appeared in the bibliography to the second edition have been omitted. Other main exclusions are many books on travel and tourism, including publications of the British Tourist Authority and national tourist boards, whose lists may be obtained from them by readers.

I wish to record again my appreciation to those who in one way and another influenced my thinking about hotels and this book, and to express the hope that the new edition may serve the needs of students, teachers and practitioners as well as the earlier editions appear to have done. I am also indebted to Horwath International for the data provided in their reports on hotel operations and to the following who supplied material used in the preparation of the new edition:

Accor, *Caterer & Hotelkeeper*, Forte PLC, Martin Gerty, Holiday Inn Worldwide, *Hotels*, Inter-Continental Hotels, Sonesta Hotels & Resorts, Swallow Hotels, Graham Wason, Whitbread Group of Hotels.

*Guildford 1994*                                                    *S. Medlik*

# PART I

Basic Hotel Concepts

# 1 *Staying Away from Home*

For the greater part of each year most people live at home.
Although they may go to work, shopping, visiting friends and
relatives, and take part in other social and leisure activities, their
homes are where they normally return each day and where they
spend the night. But many of them also increasingly stay away from
home, on business or on holiday or for other reasons, throughout
the year. Many of them stay in hotels.

Walking through a town, there are the shops, offices, workshops,
restaurants, and a whole host of other places of work,
entertainment and recreation. Driving through the country, one
passes factories, farms, petrol stations. Without going too far in the
town or in the country, one building emerges sooner or later from
the rest - an hotel.

The people one meets in the town and in the country are
residents or visitors. The places they frequent often serve primarily
the needs of the resident population, but in many areas to which
visitors go in large numbers, many of the facilities and amenities
are provided mainly for visitors. One of them invariably owes its
origin to visitors – the hotel. To a greater or lesser extent hotel
restaurants, bars and other hotel facilities may also serve the local
population, but the primary function of an hotel is to accommodate
those away from home and to supply them with their basic needs.

It is the basic function of the hotel, which makes it quite distinct
from other types of business, and to which its other functions are
supplementary. Where others provide accommodation, meals and
refreshments for those away from home – such as hospitals or
boarding schools, or hostels, their primary purpose – whether
treatment or education or something else – is different. Also in

practice it is not difficult to draw a line between the provision of accommodation by hotels and the letting of accommodation on a tenancy basis, but more difficult between hotels and guest houses and similar establishments, which share the basic function of the hotel. However, it is sufficient for our purposes to describe an hotel as an establishment providing for reward accommodation, food and drink for travellers and temporary residents, and usually also meals and refreshments and sometimes other facilities for other users.

## The Importance of Hotels

Hotels play an important role in most countries in *providing facilities* for the transaction of business, for meetings and conferences, for recreation and entertainment. In that sense hotels are as essential to economies and societies as are adequate transport, communication and retail distribution systems for various goods and services. Through their facilities hotels contribute to the total output of goods and services, which makes up the material well-being of nations and communities.

In many areas hotels are important *attractions for visitors* who bring to them spending power and who tend to spend at a higher rate than they do when they are at home. Through visitor spending hotels thus often contribute significantly to local economies both directly, and indirectly through the subsequent diffusion of the visitor expenditure to other recipients in the community.

In areas receiving foreign visitors, hotels are often important *foreign currency earners* and in this way may contribute significantly to their countries' balance of payments. Particularly in countries with limited export possibilities, hotels may be one of the few sources of foreign currency earnings.

Hotels are important *employers of labour*. Thousands of jobs are provided by hotels in the many occupations that make up the hotel industries in most countries; many others in the industry are self–employed and proprietors of smaller hotels. The role of hotels as employers is particularly important in areas with few alternative sources of employment, where they contribute to regional development.

Hotels are also important *outlets for the products of other industries*. In the building and modernization of hotels business is provided for the construction industry and related trades. Equipment, furniture and furnishings are supplied to hotels by a wide range of manufacturers. Food, drink and other consumables are among the most significant daily hotel purchases from farmers, fishermen, food and drink suppliers, and from gas, electricity and water undertakings. In addition to those engaged directly in hotels, much indirect employment is, therefore, generated by hotels for those employed in industries supplying them.

Last but not least, hotels are an important *source of amenities for local residents*. Their restaurants, bars and other facilities often attract much local custom and many hotels have become social centres of their communities.

---

British Hotel Industry 1980–1990

- Over the 1980s hotel industry sales grew faster than the Gross National Product (GNP). Between 1980 and 1990 the industry turnover increased 156 per cent compared with 139 per cent increase in GNP. The hotel industry growth in turnover also exceeded the growth in GNP in real terms (44 per cent against 31 per cent).
- The hotel industry created more than 50,000 jobs between 1982 and 1990, more than three times the rate of job creation in the whole economy.

(Appendix A)

---

US Hotel Industry 1980–1990

- Over the 1980s hotel industry sales grew faster than the Gross National Product (GNP). Between 1980 and 1990 hotel industry receipts increased 125 per cent compared with 100 per cent increase in GNP. The hotel industry growth in receipts also exceeded the growth in GNP in real terms (36 per cent against 33 per cent).
- The hotel industry created more than half a million jobs (+ 54 per cent), two-and-a-half times the rate of job creation for all US industries (+ 22 per cent).

(Appendix B)

## Travel and Hotels

Staying away from home is a function of travel and three main phases may be distinguished in the development of travel in the northern hemisphere (Figure 1).

| Circa 1850 | | Circa 1950 |
|---|---|---|
| Stage coach | Railway<br>Steamship | Motor car<br>Aircraft |
| Inns | Hotels<br>Guest houses<br>Boarding houses | Hotels/motels<br>Holiday centres<br>Other self-catering |

**Figure 1**  Three Phases of Travel

*Until about the middle of the nineteenth century* the bulk of journeys were undertaken for business and vocational reasons, by road, by people travelling mainly in their own countries. The volume of travel was relatively small, confined to a small fraction of the population in any country, and most of those who did travel, did so by coach. Inns and similar hostelries along the highways and in the principal towns provided the means of accommodation well into the nineteenth century.

*Between about 1850 and about 1950* a growing proportion of travellers went away from home for other than business reasons and holidays came to represent gradually an important reason for a journey. For a hundred years or so, the railway and the steamship dominated passenger transportation, and the new means of transport gave an impetus to travel between countries and between continents. Although the first hotels date from the eighteenth century, their growth on any scale occurred only in the nineteenth century, when first the railway and later the steamship created sufficiently large markets to make the larger hotel possible. Hotels together with guest houses and boarding houses dominated the accommodation market in this period.

By *about the middle of the twentieth century* in most developed countries of the world (a little earlier in North America and a little later in Europe) a whole cycle was completed and most traffic returned to the road, with the motor car increasingly providing the main means of passenger transportation. Almost concurrently the aircraft took over unmistakably both from the railways and from shipping as the principal means of long-distance passenger transport. On many routes holiday traffic came to match and often greatly exceed other traffic. A growing volume of travel away from home became international. Hotels entered into competition with new forms of accommodation – holiday centres and holiday villages in Europe, motels in North America, and various self–catering facilities for those on holiday.

## Two Centuries of Hotelkeeping

Hotels are some two hundred years old. The word 'hotel' itself came into use in *England* with the introduction in London, after 1760, of the kind of establishment then common in Paris, called 'hôtel garni', or a large house, in which apartments were let by the day, week or month. Its appearance signified a departure from the customary method of accommodating guests in inns and similar hostelries, into something more luxurious and even ostentatious. Hotels with managers, receptionists and uniformed staff arrived generally only at the beginning of the nineteenth century and until the middle of that century their development was relatively slow. The absence of good inns in *Scotland* to some extent accelerated the arrival of the hotel there; by the end of the eighteenth century Edinburgh, for example, had several hotels where the traveller could get elegant and comfortable rooms. Hotels are also known to have made much progress in other parts of *Europe* in the closing years of the eighteenth and early years of the nineteenth century, where at the time originated the idea of a resort hotel.

In *North America* early accommodation for travellers followed a similar pattern as in England, with most inns originating in converted houses, but by the turn of the eighteenth century several cities on the eastern seaboard had purpose–built hotels and in the first half of the nineteenth century hotel building spread across America to the Pacific Coast. The evolution from innkeeping to hotelkeeping, therefore, proceeded almost in parallel in the Old and in the New Worlds and the rise of the hotel industries on both sides of the Atlantic had probably more in common than is generally recognized. What America might have lacked in history and tradition, it more than made up in pioneering spirit, in intense rivalry between cities and entrepreneurs, and in the sheer size and growth of the travel market.

In the last century hotels became firmly established not only as centres of commercial hospitality for travellers, but often also as important social centres of their communities. Their building, management and operation became specialized activities, with their own styles and methods. The present century brought about growing specialization and increased sophistication in the hotel industries of most countries, as well as their growth and expansion. But the growth and the diversity of hotel operations has been also matched by the growth and diversity of competition in the total accommodation market.

## Hotels in the Total Accommodation Market

In any country the demand for accommodation away from home is generated by residents travelling in their own country and by foreign visitors. In developed countries most travel tends to be by the residents for leisure purposes. In developing countries most travel by residents is on business but they also often receive many leisure visitors from abroad.

**Table 1**
Accommodation Profile of Selected European Countries, 1990

| Ratio of beds | Hotels and similar establishments[a] | Supplementary accommodation[b] |
| --- | --- | --- |
| Austria | 56 | 44[e] |
| Belgium | 17 | 83[d] |
| France (1991) | 27 | 73[d] |
| Germany[c] | 66 | 34[e] |
| Greece (1989) | 58 | 42 |
| Portugal | 40 | 60[d] |
| Sweden | 26 | 74[d] |
| Switzerland | 24 | 76 |
| Turkey | 81 | 19[d] |

| Ratio of nights spent in all establishments | By foreign visitors | By domestic visitors |
| --- | --- | --- |
| Austria | 77 | 23 |
| Belgium | 35 | 65 |
| France | 36 | 64 |
| Germany[f] | 14 | 86 |
| Greece | 75 | 25 |
| Portugal | 59 | 41 |
| Sweden | 20 | 80 |
| Switzerland | 49 | 51 |
| Turkey | 66 | 34 |

[a] For most countries, hotels and similar establishments include hotels, motels, inns and boarding houses.
[b] Supplementary accommodation includes variously youth hostels, holiday villages, rented rooms, houses and flats, camping sites.
[c] The data relate to the territory of the Federal Republic of Germany prior to 3 October 1990.
[d] Excluding rented rooms, houses and flats.
[e] Excluding camping sites.
[f] The data relate to the territory of the Federal Republic of Germany to 3 October 1990; from the unification visitors from the former German Democratic Republic are regarded as domestic visitors.
*Source*: Based on Organisation for Economic Co–operation and Development, *Tourism Policy and International Tourism in OECD Member Countries 1990–1991*.

Information about accommodation facilities in individual countries essentially reflects the designations used for them by the countries concerned and the coverage of various types in the available statistics. Only very broad inter-country comparisons are possible. One source is the annual report of the Tourism Committee of the Organisation for Economic Co-operation and Development (OECD), which distinguishes between beds available in hotels and similar establishments, and in what is described as supplementary accommodation.

The ratio of beds in hotels and similar establishments to beds in supplementary accommodation gives an indication of the relative importance of the hotel sector in the total accommodation market of individual countries, as shown in Table 1. In most countries the accommodation profile tends to reflect the relative importance of foreign and domestic users, of leisure and business travel, and of other influences. In many countries hotels and similar establishments appear to be minority providers of accommodation.

- According to the World Tourism Organization (WTO) there are 12.25 million rooms or 22.4 million beds in hotels and similar establishments worldwide.
- Around one-half of the world total is in Europe and well over one-half of the European capacity is located in five countries – Italy, Germany, Spain, France and the United Kingdom.
- United States account for three-quarters of the rooms and two–thirds of the beds in the Americas.
- China has almost one-quarter and, together with Japan, Thailand and Australia, more than two–thirds of the total capacity in East Asia and the Pacific.
- The remaining global regions – Africa, Middle East and South Asia – combined have only 5-6 per cent of the world total.

(Appendix C)

## Hotel Location

Hotel services are supplied to their buyers direct in person; they are consumed at the point of sale, and they are also produced there. Hotel services must be, therefore, provided where the demand exists and the market is the dominant influence on hotel location. In fact, location is part of the hotel product. In turn, location is the key influence on the viability of the business, so much so that a prominent entrepreneur could have said with conviction and with much justification that there are only three rules for success in the hotel business: location, location, location.

We have seen earlier that from the early days all accommodation units followed *transport* modes. Inns and other hostelries were situated along the roads and at destinations, serving transit and terminal traffic. The rapid spread of railways marked the emergence of railway hotels in the nineteenth century. In the twentieth century motor transport created a new demand for accommodation along the highways and the modern motel and motor hotel have been distinctive responses to the new impetus of the motor car. A similar but less pronounced influence was passenger shipping, which stimulated hotel development in ports, and more recently air transport, which brought about a major growth of hotels in the vicinity of airports and air terminals.

Secondly, although this is closely related to transport, many hotels are located to serve first and foremost *holiday* markets. In their areas of highest concentration, holiday visitors are accommodated in hotels in localities where the resident population may represent only a small proportion of those present at the time, as is the case in many resorts.

The third major influence on hotel location is the location of *economic activity*, and of industry and commerce in particular. Whilst again not separable from transport development, industrial and commercial activities create demand for transit and terminal accommodation in industrial and commercial centres, in locations not frequented by holiday visitors.

Different segments of the travel market give rise to distinctive patterns of demand for hotel accommodation and often distinctive types of hotels. In business and industrial centres hotels normally achieve their highest occupancies on weekdays and in resorts in the main holiday seasons; their facilities and services reflect the requirements of businessmen and of holiday visitors respectively. Between these clearly defined segments come other towns and areas, such as busy commercial centres with historical or other attractions for visitors, which may achieve a more even weekly and annual pattern of business.

## Types of Hotels

The rich variety of hotels can be seen from the many terms in use to denote particular types. Hotels are referred to as luxury, resort,

commercial, residential, transit, and in many other ways. Each of
these terms may give an indication of standard or location, or
particular type of guest who makes up most of the market of a
particular hotel, but it does not describe adequately its main
characteristics. These can be only seen when a combination of
terms is applied to an hotel, each of which describes a particular
hotel according to certain criteria. It is helpful to appreciate at this
stage what the main types of hotels are, by adopting particular
criteria for classifying them, without necessarily attaching precise
meanings to them.

Thus according to *location* hotels are in cities and in large and
small towns, in inland, coastal and mountain resorts, and in
the country.

According to the actual *position* of the hotel in its location it
may be in the city or town centre or in the suburbs, along the
beach of a coastal resort, along the highway.

By reference to its relationship with particular means of
*transport* there are motels and motor hotels, railway hotels,
airport hotels (the terms also indicating location).

According to the *purpose of visit* and the main reason for their
guests' stay, hotels may become known as business hotels,
holiday hotels, convention hotels, tourist hotels.

Where there is a pronounced tendency to a *short or long
duration* of guests' stay, it may be an important hotel
characteristic, so that the hotel becomes a transit or a
residential hotel.

According to the *range of its facilities and services* an hotel may
be open to residents and non-residents, or it may restrict itself
to providing overnight accommodation and at most offering
breakfast to its guests, and be an hôtel garni or apartment
hotel.

Whether an hotel holds a *licence* for the sale of alcoholic liquor
or not, is an important dimension in the range of available
hotel services, and the distinction between licensed and
unlicensed hotels is, therefore, of relevance in describing an
hotel in most countries.

There is no universal agreement on how hotels should be
described according to *size*, but by reference to their room or
bed capacities we normally apply the term small hotel to one
with a small amount of sleeping accommodation, the term
large hotel to one with several hundred beds or bedrooms, and

the term medium-sized hotel to one somewhere between the two, according to the size structure of the hotel industry in a particular country.

● Whatever the criteria used in hotel guides and in classification and grading systems in existence in many countries, normally at least four or five classes or grades have been found necessary to distinguish adequately in the standards of hotels and these have found some currency among hotel users. The extremes of luxury and basic standards, sometimes denoted by five stars and one star respectively are not difficult concepts; the mid–point on any such scale denotes the average without any particular claims to merit. The intervening points are then standards above average but falling short of luxury (quality hotels) and standards above basic (economy).

● Last but not least comes the *ownership and management*. Individually owned independent hotels, which may be managed by the proprietor or by a salaried manager, have to be distinguished from chain or group hotels, invariably owned by a company. Independent hotels may belong to an hotel consortium or cooperative. A company may operate its hotels under direct management or under a franchise agreement.

The above distinctions then enable us to describe a particular hotel in broad terms, concisely, comprehensively and meaningfully, e.g.:

● Terminus Hotel is a medium-sized economy town centre unlicensed hotel, owned and managed by a small company, catering mainly for tourists visiting the historic town and the surrounding countryside.

● Hotel Excelsior is a large independent luxury hotel on the main promenade of the coastal resort, with holiday visitors as its main market.

● The Crossroads Hotel is a small licensed quality transit motor hotel, operated as a franchise, on the outskirts of the city, which serves mainly travelling businessmen and tourists.

## A Review So Far

In this chapter hotels are described as businesses of commercial hospitality, which play an important role in many of the economies and societies, in which they operate. Three phases are distinguished in the evolution of travel and accommodation away from home and the development of hotels is traced to their beginnings some two hundred years ago. However, hotels are not the only providers of accommodation and compete with others in the accommodation market. Their location has been determined by developments in transport, holidays and economic activity. These and other influences have given rise to different types of hotels, which can be described in terms of their principal characteristics. In the next chapter they are viewed in terms of their products and markets.

The aim of this chapter* is to outline the facilities and services provided by hotels, who are the people who use hotels, why they use hotels, and what influences their choice of particular hotels. In providing answers to these questions, we can formulate a conceptual model of an hotel, which attempts to explain in simple terms how particular hotel products meet the needs of particular hotel markets, and establish a basis for a more detailed examination of the hotel business in subsequent chapters.

## The Hotel as a Total Market Concept

From the point of view of its users, an hotel is an institution of commercial hospitality, which offers its facilities and services for sale, individually or in various combinations, and this concept is made up of several elements, as shown in Figure 2.

Its *location* places the hotel geographically in or near a particular city, town or village; within a given area location denotes accessibility and the convenience this represents, attractiveness of surroundings and the appeal this represents, freedom from noise and other nuisances, or otherwise.

Its *facilities*, which include bedrooms, restaurants, bars, function rooms, meeting rooms and recreation facilities such as tennis courts and swimming pools, represent a repertoire of facilities for the use of its customers, and these may be differentiated in type, size, and in other ways.

* This chapter reflects in particular the work of Roger Doswell as Kobler Research Fellow at the University of Surrey in the late 1960s.

**Figure 2**   The Hotel as a Market Concept

Its *service* comprises the availability and extent of particular hotel services provided through its facilities; the style and quality of all these in such terms as formality and informality, degree of personal attention, and speed and efficiency.

Its *image* may be defined as the way in which the hotel portrays itself to people and the way in which it is perceived as portraying itself by them. It is a byproduct of its location, facilities and service, but it is enhanced by such factors as its name, appearance, atmosphere; its associations – by who stays there and who eats there; by what it says about itself and what other people say about it.

Its *price* expresses the value given by the hotel through its location, facilities, service and image, and the satisfaction derived by its users from these elements of the hotel concept.

The individual elements assume greater or lesser importance for different people. One person may put location as paramount and be prepared to accept basic facilities and service for an overnight stay, ignoring the image, as long as the price is within a limit, to which he is willing to go. Another may be more concerned with the image of the hotel, its facilities and service. However, all the five elements are related to each other, and in a situation of choice most hotel users tend either to accept or reject an hotel as a whole, that is the total concept.

There are varying degrees of adaptability and flexibility in the total hotel concept, ranging from the complete fixity of its location to the relative flexibility of price, with facilities, service and image lending themselves to some adaptation in particular circumstances with time.

> The issue of the future is the extent to which personal service will be expected and should be provided. In hotels which are concentrating on providing a reduced number of facilities and a greater level of guest self-service, personal service can and will be reduced, perhaps also utilising technological advancements for this purpose. But in hotels providing a high level of personal service, technological advancements will be harnessed to improve the service, rather than to reduce the level of staffing.
>
> Horwath and Horwath, *Hotels of the Future*

## Hotel Facilities and Services as Products

In the early days of innkeeping the traveller often had to bring his own food to places where he stayed the night – bed for the night was the only product offered. But soon most establishments extended their hospitality to providing at least some food and refreshments. Today many apartment hotels, hôtels garni, and motels confine their facilities to sleeping accommodation, with little or no catering provision. But the typical hotel as we know it today, normally provides not only accommodation, but also food and drink, and sometimes other facilities and services, and makes them available not only to its residents but also to non-residents. This is the concept which will be developed in this chapter and in later parts of this book.

Although the range of hotel facilities and services may extend as far as to cater for all or most needs of their customers, however long their stay, and for an hotel to become a self-contained community with its own shops, entertainments and recreation facilities, it is helpful at this stage to describe the hotel concept in a simpler form, by including only the main customer needs typically met by most hotels.

The main customer demand in most hotels is for sleeping accommodation, food and drink, and for food and drink for organized groups. These four requirements then relate to accommodation, restaurants, bars and functions, as the principal hotel products.

Sleeping accommodation is provided for hotel residents alone. Restaurants and bars meet the requirements of hotel residents and non-residents alike, even though separate facilities may be sometimes provided for them. Functions are best seen as a separate hotel product bought by organized groups; these groups may be resident in the hotel as, for example, participants in a residential conference, or be non-residents, such as a local club or society, or the group may combine the two.

The total hotel concept – of location, facilities, service, image and price – can be, therefore, sub-divided according to the needs of the customer and the particular facilities brought into play to meet them. The cluster of elements of the total hotel concept is then related to each particular hotel product. Each hotel product contains the elements of the location, facilities, services, image and price, to meet a particular customer need or set of needs. The first approach to the segmentation of the hotel market is, therefore, taken by dividing hotel users according to the products bought. Corresponding to each hotel product there are the buyers of that product who constitute a market for it.

## Hotel Accommodation Markets

Hotel users who are buyers of overnight accommodation may be classified according to the main purpose of their visit to a particular location into three main categories as holiday, business and other users.

*Holiday users* include a variety of leisure travel as the main reason for their stay in hotels, ranging from short stays in a particular location on the way to somewhere else to weekend and longer stays when the location represents the end of a journey. Their demand for hotel accommodation tends to be resort-oriented, seasonal and sensitive to price.

*Business users* are employees and others travelling in the course of their work, people visiting exhibitions, trade fairs, or coming together as members of professional and commercial organizations for meetings and conferences. Their demand for hotel accommodation tends to be town- and city-oriented, non-seasonal and less price-sensitive, except in the case of some event attractions such as conferences and exhibitions, which may be usefully regarded as a separate category.

*Other hotel users* comprise visitors to a particular location for a variety of reasons other than holiday or business, e.g. those attending such family occasions as weddings, parents visiting educational institutions, visitors to special events, and common interest groups meeting for other than business and vocational reasons, re-locating families and individuals seeking permanent accommodation in an area and staying temporarily in an hotel, people living in an hotel permanently. The characteristics of this type of demand are more varied than those of the first and second group, and it is, therefore, often desirable to sub-divide it further for practical purposes.

Within and between the three main groups, which comprise the total market for hotel accommodation, there are several distinctions important to individual hotels. We have noted already that some hotel users give rise to demand for transit and short-stay accommodation, others are terminal visitors with a longer average stay. Also, for example, much business demand is generated by a relatively small number of travellers who are frequent hotel users; most holiday and other demand comes from a very large number of people who use hotels only occasionally. Moreover, business users often book accommodation at short notice, whilst holiday and other users tend to do so longer in advance. And in all three groups some people are individual hotel users, and others stay in hotels in groups.

## Hotel Catering Markets

Hotel restaurants, bars and function rooms may be conveniently grouped together as its food and beverage or catering facilities, and the meals and refreshments they provide as the hotel food and beverage or catering products. Corresponding to them there are again buyers of these products who constitute the hotel catering markets and who may be classified in various ways. For our purposes there is a basic distinction between the demand exercised by hotel residents, by non-residents, and by organized groups.

The first category of users of hotel restaurants and bars is related to the basic function of the hotel in providing overnight sleeping accommodation, and consists of *hotel residents*, whom we have classified earlier as holiday, business and other users. Their use of hotel catering facilities tends to be influenced by the reason for their hotel stay and by the terms on which they stay. Breakfast is their common hotel purchase, but otherwise an hotel resident may have his meals in his hotel or elsewhere, and he is more likely to be an hotel restaurant or bar customer in the evenings than at midday.

The second category are *non-residents*, individually or in small groups, when eating out. They may, in fact, be staying at other hotels or accommodation establishments or with friends or relatives or be day visitors to the area, for holiday, business or other reasons.

Alternatively they are local residents, for whom the hotel restaurants and bars represent outlets for meals and refreshments, as a leisure activity or as part of their business activities. This category tends to represent important hotel users at midday as well as in the evenings, particularly at weekends.

The third category of users of hotel catering facilities are *organized groups* who make advance arrangements for functions at the hotel, which may call for separate facilities and organizational arrangements. They include local clubs, societies, business and professional groups, as well as participants in meetings and conferences originating from outside the area.

Hotel catering products represent a greater diversity than its accommodation products and it is often correspondingly more difficult to classify them and the markets for them in practice. Moreover, hotels are not alone in supplying them. In the market for meals and refreshments for individuals and groups an hotel competes not only with other hotels, but also with restaurants outside hotels, pubs and clubs, to name but a few other types of outlet. Therefore, catering in hotels is a separate hotel function, with its own objectives, policies and strategies, and with its own organization.

## Hotel Demand Generating Sources

For most people the use of hotels represents what is known as derived demand because few stay or eat in hotels for its own sake; their primary reasons for doing so lie in their reasons for visiting an area or for spending their time there in particular ways. When describing hotel accommodation and catering markets we have seen that hotel users have different degrees of freedom and choice as to whether they buy hotel services or not. Some have few or no alternatives; for them only hotels provide the facilities and services which they require in a particular area in pursuit of their business, vocational and other interests; the incidence of their hotel usage arises to a great extent from their working circumstances. For many others the use of hotels is a matter of choice; they do so in their pursuit of leisure and recreation; for them hotel usage involves a discretionary use of their time and money. This distinction helps us identify the demand generating sources for hotels in a given area, which are of three main types – institutional, recreational and transit.

*Institutional* sources include industrial and commercial enterprises, educational institutions, government establishments and other organizations in the private and public sector, whose activities are involved in the economic life of the community and in its administration. These institutions generate demand for hotels through their own visitors and their other requirements for hotel facilities and services.

*Recreational* sources include historical, scenic and other site attractions and event attractions, which generate demand for hotels from tourists; local events and activities in the social and cultural life of the community, which generate demand from clubs, societies and other organizations; happenings of significance to individuals and families.

The third source of demand stems from individuals and groups with no intrinsic reason for spending time in a particular locality, other than being on the way somewhere else and the need to break a journey. This source of demand is closely related to particular forms of transport, it expresses itself on highways, at ports and at airports, and may be described as *transit*.

It will be readily apparent that this view of demand generating sources for hotels is closely related to several aspects of the hotel business considered earlier – for example, to the three-fold classification of the hotel accommodation market into holiday, business and other users; to the three main influences on hotel location – travel, holidays and economic activity; and to the types of hotel distinguished in Chapter 1. By adopting in each case a somewhat different viewpoint, it is possible to highlight the interdependence between the location, markets and products of hotels.

## Hotel Market Areas

We can define an hotel market in several ways – by reference to the people who buy hotel services, as a network of dealings between the hotel and its users, or as an area which an hotel serves. In the first two approaches hotel users may come from within the area, from various parts of the country, and from abroad; we then refer to the local, domestic and foreign markets, and subdivide them in appropriate ways. In the third approach described below we view the hotel market area as a physical area served by the hotel.

*For hotel accommodation* it is necessary to identify all the institutional and recreational sources of demand, which may be served by a particular hotel. The area drawn in this way round the hotel may extend from its immediate vicinity to a radius of several miles or more. How far it does extend, depends on the geographical distribution of the demand generating sources, the mode of transport used by the hotel users of each source, and the availability of other facilities in the area. The head office of a large firm, a university, an historic castle, and a town which is a festival centre, may be all within a market area of an hotel, if the hotel is reasonably accessible from these points, and if its location at least matches the location of other hotels. The market area may coincide for a number of hotels within close proximity of each other, which offer a similar concept in terms of facilities, service, image and price. On the periphery the market area for an hotel may overlap with the market areas of other hotels some distance away. At periods of peak demand it may extend further than at times of low demand. For transit the accommodation market area is related to the journeys undertaken through the area – their origin and destination, the method of transportation, the time of day, the time of year and other circumstances of the journeys.

*For hotel catering services* the market area depends on market density – the availability of spending power within an area, as well as on the accessibility of the hotel to the different sources of demand, and on the availability of other catering services in the area. In this there is a close analogy with the concept of a catchment area for other retail outlets, as far as the resident population is concerned. How far do people go from where they live to do their shopping? The distance may vary according to the purchase they are to make. Similarly there may be a smaller market area for hotel lunches than for hotel dinners and functions, because close proximity to the hotel may be a more important consideration for a midday meal than for an evening out.

## Hotel Market Segmentation

The market for hotel products may be divided into several components or segments and this enables individual hotels to identify their actual and potential users according to various criteria. Segmentation then provides a basis for the marketing of hotel products, for paying close attention to the requirements of different users, and for monitoring the performance in the markets chosen by an hotel.

Earlier in this chapter we divided hotel users, according to the product bought by them, into buyers of accommodation, food, drink and functions. We divided the accommodation market, according to the reasons for the users' stay, into holiday, business and other users, and the hotel catering market into hotel residents, non-residents and functions. According to the origin of demand we also identified institutional, recreational and transit sources of demand. Another basis for segmentation is the needs of hotel users and the means they have to pay for their satisfaction, by dividing them according to their socio-economic characteristics. Socio-economic classifications seek to group people according to their occupation and employment status. For example, the British Joint Industry Committee for National Readership Surveys (JICNARS) defines social grades as shown in Table 2.

**Table 2**
Social Grade Definitions

| Social grade | Social status | Occupation |
| --- | --- | --- |
| A | Upper middle class | Higher managerial, administrative or professional |
| B | Middle class | Intermediate managerial, administrative or professional |
| C1 | Lower middle class | Supervisory or clerical, and junior managerial, administrative or professional |
| C2 | Skilled working class | Skilled manual workers |
| D | Working class | Semi- and unskilled manual |
| E | Those at the lowest level of subsistence | State pensioners or widows (no other earner), casual or lowest grade workers |

The grades may be applied to hotel users and to the grades of hotels postulated in Chapter 1. Social grade A might be expected to stay in luxury and quality hotels, B in medium hotels, C in economy hotels. However, this is an oversimplification, because the same people may interchange between segments according to the circumstances in which they find themselves. A businessman on an expense account may stay in a quality hotel, but travelling for pleasure with his family he may stay in a lower grade hotel. Moreover, the incidence of hotel usage among DE groups is minimal. Nevertheless, segmentation by socio-economic criteria is an important approach to market segmentation. For some purposes age, family composition, life cycle stage, or other criteria may be more appropriate.

A concomitant of market segmentation is product branding, with a view to differentiating an hotel from others in the minds of buyers, long established in other consumer industries. Some hotel groups have focused on branded segments distinguished by levels of service; examples include Holiday Inn upmarket Crowne Plaza, core brand Holiday Inn and limited service Garden Court. Other brands have been created by grouping like operations, such as Forte Posthouses and Whitbread Lansbury Hotels, or by acquisition, such as Forte Crest and Mount Charlotte Thistle.

> We anticipate that product segmentation will assume even greater significance in the future development of hotel companies. It is an effective method for hotel companies to maintain or expand market share and in some instances create new markets.
>
> Product branding will become more focussed and will reflect increasing levels of segmentation.
>
> In the light of this, the future of the 'all purpose hotel' is doubtful in terms of its competitiveness in the market place.
>
> The greatest growth potential sectors seem to be the high quality all-suite unit and the economy hotel – i.e. at the high and low end of the market.
>
> Horwath and Horwath, *Hotels of the Future*

## Buying and Paying for Hotel Services

It is important to understand how a buying decision is made, who makes it, and who pays for the hotel services bought.

*The buying decision* itself may be basically of two kinds – *deliberate* or *impulsive*. Before embarking on journeys, business people may ask secretaries to reserve hotel rooms in the towns they are to visit for specified nights. A family may arrive at their choice of holiday hotel after a scrutiny of hotel guides. A society may make several inquiries before choosing the venue for their annual dinner dance. These are deliberate buying decisions made with some advance planning and with advance reservations. A tourist looking for somewhere to stay when travelling by car, or on arrival at the railway station or airport, is likely to make an impulse decision, in much the same way as a couple walking through the streets of a town and 'discovering' a restaurant which appears to be to their liking. Purchases of hotel products are both deliberate and impulse purchases and most hotels respond to both, although different operational policies and procedures normally apply to each.

Many people make their own arrangements for travelling and for staying in hotels. However, many hotel bookings are made by people who do it for others: the secretary for the boss, the travel agent for the client, the business travel department of a large company for its employees. In these circumstances it is important to know who *the buying agent* is and where that person is located, if the knowledge derived from the analysis of the hotel demand generating sources is to be applied to bringing about sales. Most hotels can no longer hope to fill their beds, restaurants and bars by simply waiting for the guest.

According to the *source of payment* for hotel services, hotel users are also of two basic kinds – those who pay themselves and those whose hotel bills are covered or reimbursed for them. Most leisure use of hotels represents personal expenditure out of disposable incomes, the bulk of business use of hotels in the wide sense is paid for directly or indirectly by third parties – employers and other agencies on behalf of the guest. Although many business users have no fixed limits as to the charges they incur in hotels, many tend to observe what they and their organizations regard as acceptable. The understanding of these practices is important to hotels too. The decision on the market segments to be catered for is closely related to decisions on pricing and we have seen that price is an integral element of each hotel's total concept.

## Hotel Marketing Orientation

Hotels serve people and their success depends on how well they serve them in places where they wish to be served. This is only a way of stating in the simplest of terms the application to hotel operations of the marketing concept, which is concerned with the consumer as a starting point in the conduct of business.

The marketing concept is beginning to be understood by hoteliers. Although some continue to regard sales and marketing as synonymous, most hotels no longer operate in the seller's market and even massive sales effort is not likely to generate a sustained high volume of business, if consumer needs are not genuinely met in the planning, design and subsequent operation of an hotel.

The basic hotel concept outlined at the beginning of this chapter stresses the view of the hotel, as it is seen by the hotel user rather than the hotel operator, as a business to meet the needs of hotel users. Some of these needs are basic and physical, such as sleeping in clean beds or eating wholesome meals; others such as those met by the image of the hotel are acquired needs, which reflect what a person aims to be as an individual. A successful hotel must seek to meet both sets of needs.

So that an hotel can meet the needs of hotel users, individual hotel services have to be seen as hotel products sold to particular markets. An hotel cannot be all things to all people. Each hotel has to achieve a match between its particular products and particular market segments, i.e. groups of people with more or less similar characteristics and requirements for hotel services. In this there is a difference between the hotel accommodation and catering products, in that each may to some extent cater for different markets. But this difference only reinforces the need for harmony in the total hotel concept. In order to achieve the match between hotel products and markets, there is a need for a careful analysis of the sources of demand for hotel services in the market area served by the hotel and an understanding of how hotel services are bought and paid for.

From this model of an hotel a translation can be made to particular operations. This takes the form of hotel policies, philosophies and strategies, which are discussed in the next chapter. The role and scope of the marketing function in hotels is considered in Chapter 10.

Marketing in the hotel industry is in the process of rapid change. Demographic and social evolution is causing fundamental changes in the available markets, the customer profiles, and the generating countries and regions. Technological development, at a pace inconceivable to previous generations, is and will be causing fundamental changes in ways in which hotels reach their customers and potential customers choose their hotels.

The principles remain the same. The hotelier must know his potential market opportunities, must select the ones appropriate to the product he can offer profitably, must ensure that his product is suitable to this market, and then must target his marketing and selling accordingly and cost-effectively.

Horwath and Horwath, *Hotels of the Future*

# Hotel Policies, Philosophies and Strategies

'I am an owner of the leading hotel in a provincial town, which has been in my family for three generations. We cater for businessmen staying in the town, local business and professional people using our restaurant and bar, and various societies and other organizations holding functions in our banqueting room. We are well known for the quality of what we provide, our prices reflect this, and our main objective is to maintain and enhance our position and profitability against increasing competition, especially for lunch and dinner business. We aim to retain the loyalty of our customers through our personal service, our staff by being the best hotel employer in the town, and our suppliers by giving them a fair deal.'

'We are in business to provide a chain of economy motels for low-spending tourists, businessmen with modest allowances, and other travellers with limited budgets, who look for basic facilities at low prices. To achieve profitability in this market, our motels are only in locations where we can achieve high occupancies in most parts of the year and throughout most weeks of the year - where a high level of demand is generated by a combination of tourist, business and other traffic. They are located outside town centres where land values are low, they are purpose built for maximum efficiency, and they provide simple standards of facilities with minimum service. Through this type of operation we are aiming to meet a real market need with a high and stable volume of demand, and to provide manifestly good value for money with low operating costs, whilst generating a high level of profit for our company.'

'Our company operates quality resort hotels with good road and rail access from London and the Home Counties, and specializes in long-staying holiday visitors in the summer and smaller conferences in other parts of the year. We have grown to our present size by acquiring suitable properties in the locations we have chosen, modernizing them, and promoting them vigorously in our markets. We intend to continue growing in this way, financing further growth significantly from our own resources, as we have done from the outset. In doing this, we shall aim to give our guests hotels meeting their particular requirements, provide our employees and the resorts in which we operate with year-round employment, and earn for our shareholders a return at least comparable to what they could obtain in similar types of business.'

## Objectives and Policies

The three statements provide in varying degrees of formality and preciseness examples of how three different operators see themselves in the hotel business. They say who is involved in the business as owner (a sole trader in one case and a company in the other two); where it operates (location) and what facilities and services (products) it supplies; who are its main customers (markets). Beyond this there are further indications of what the businesses are striving to achieve (profitability, growth, customer and employee satisfaction, and in some cases also other aims). The statements also include some mention of the rationale of the approach adopted and of the means employed to achieve what they set out to do. These are some answers to the question 'What is the purpose of our hotel business?' and represent broad objectives of the three firms.

In seeking to explain why thousands earn their living by owning and operating hotels, it is tempting to say that they do it to earn a profit. But this is an oversimplification. From the point of view of the community and of hotel customers, the purpose of an hotel is to provide certain facilities and services to its users. From the point of view of its employees an hotel is a source of employment. From the point of view of its owners an hotel provides a return on their investment. These are very disparate purposes, and viewing them in this way recognizes that there is not one but at least three main parties to the hotel business, each with one or more primary objectives.

Expressed in purely financial terms, customers may have a particular interest in low prices, employees in high wages, owners in high profits. But each party has a wider concern in its participation in the hotel business. Hotel customers, for example, are also concerned with the quality of facilities and services, hotel employees with working conditions, hotel owners with the security of their investment and with other satisfactions they may derive from their role.

Some of these interests may be in conflict. It is the task of hotel management to reconcile the competing and conflicting objectives of the parties, first in the formulation of the objectives of the business, and then in its subsequent operation. The maximization of one party's objectives, be it the customers', the employees' or the owners', to the neglect of the others', is not a formula for a sustained prosperity of an hotel, or for that matter of any other business, nor can it be the sole purpose for its existence.

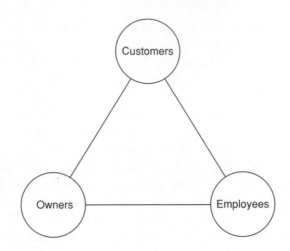

**Figure 3**  Principal Parties in the Hotel Business

At the outset, the Sonnabend family adopted a 'mission statement' that established the kind of company we wanted to be. The decision was made early on to keep the company small and manageable. To concentrate on owning, developing, and managing only a select group of unique small to medium-sized deluxe hotels of 100 to 500 rooms, in equally unique locations. To establish a collection of properties that reflect their environments rather than a cookie-cutter chain. And to dedicate our family and top management to making sure we do all of the above very well.

Roger and Paul Sonnabend, Sonesta Hotels & Resorts

● To be the preferred hotel brand by guests and the travel industry, the preferred hotel company by employees, and the preferred hotel business by developers, financial institutions, and franchisees.
● To build on the strength of the Holiday Inn name utilizing quality and consistency as the vehicles to enhance its perceived 'value for money' position in the middle market.
● To maximize distribution throughout the world by aggressive expansion of existing and new products through owned, managed and franchised developments.
● To employ our resources and investments to yield premium returns.

Holiday Inn Worldwide, The Mission Statement (1992)

- Periquito Hotels is a chain of strongly branded, mid-range hotels providing consistent standards and representing excellent value for money.

- We aim to be innovative, providing a professional and care-free environment for both guests and employees alike. Most Periquito hotels are located in town centres, and are designed to serve the needs of the business, conference and leisure guests.

- Periquito Partner Hotels are mostly independently owned and managed by Periquito Hotels Limited, providing the majority of the Periquito standards whilst still retaining some of the original features.

Periquito Hotels, Positioning Statement (1993)

## General and Sectional Policies

When an hotel has defined its objectives, its management has a focus for its actions and decisions. It is also a start in the formulation of its policies, which may be described as a set of guidelines for management. By stating the ends to be pursued and the means by which they are to be pursued, the business defines formally its attitude and approach in its dealing with customers, employees, shareholders and also with such other parties as, for example, its suppliers. In so far as this definition postulates general guidelines for the hotel as a whole, it is a *general policy*, formulated and promulgated by top management – the owner/manager in a small business, the board of directors in a company.

In order to provide adequate guidance for management decisions and actions, there is a need for more detailed guidelines in particular aspects of the business and in particular activities. These are developed as *sectional policies*, which flow from the general policy and extend it from broad policy indications into operational terms.

As the customers, employees, shareholders and suppliers are the main groups of people with whom an hotel deals, the main sectional policies are commonly formulated in relation to them to embody the principles to be observed in these relationships.

- Thus a *customer* policy normally says what the hotel is aiming to do in terms of its markets and quality standards of what it provides, includes its concept of good value and its approach to price, discounts and credit; it states its attitude to complaints and refunds.

- An *employment* or *personnel* policy covers such matters as recruitment, selection and training; remuneration, conditions of employment, welfare; promotion, retirement, termination; consultation, negotiation and the handling of disputes.
- A *shareholder* policy defines what the owners are entitled to expect in terms of their rewards, information and participation in the business, and what is expected from them.
- A policy towards *suppliers* postulates what is expected from them regarding the quality of supplies, delivery and terms, and how each can expect to be treated by the hotel.

- Swallow Hotels have an agreed minimum adult rate of pay that covers all staff. It is our policy that any worker under 21 years old who is employed to do an adult's job receives this minimum rate of pay.

- Our policy, as far as possible, is to fill vacancies by transfer and promotion within the Company. Situations vacant at hotels within the Company are circulated regularly and posted on staff notice boards.

- Some hotels offer accommodation for employees as part of their contract. However, it is the policy of Swallow Hotels to encourage their employees to live in their own accommodation away from hotels. This policy will be pursued where possible in the belief that management and staff will perform better in their tasks and enjoy, to a greater degree, both domestic and leisure activities. However, some employees may be requested to 'live in' as part of their employment contract.

- It is Swallow Hotels' policy to provide employees the skills and knowledge necessary for the Company's present and future needs. Employees will develop in an environment that will encourage career patterns to achieve higher standards, improved productivity and profitability. This in turn will ensure a higher earning potential and security of employment. It is the responsibility of the Personnel and Training Manager to identify the Company's overall training needs, which will incorporate an annual training plan.

- It is the right of each individual employee to decide whether or not to subscribe to the trade union, according to his or her own particular circumstances and beliefs. Certain arrangements have been discussed with trade unions for specific hotels and details are available in those hotels.

Extracts from Swallow Hotels *Employee's Handbook* (1993)

Sectional policies defined by reference to the main parties in the internal and external relationships of the hotel are a logical and most helpful basis of providing guidelines. However, for many situations guidelines are required also in the discharge of *functional* responsibilities of the hotel, for example in such specialist areas as financial management, marketing and purchasing. Financial management may enter into all the four relationships described above and elements of financial guidelines may be incorporated into each. A marketing policy may be viewed as an extension of a customer policy and a purchasing policy as an extension of a policy to suppliers. But it is often helpful in practice to subject these functional areas to policy guidelines of their own.

A third dimension in sectional policies arises in the existence of guidelines relating to each main hotel product – accommodation, food and drink, and functions. These may be viewed again as an extension of the hotel's customer policy, but it is often helpful in practice to state the principles on which these individual activities are to operate for the guidance of those concerned separately and in some detail. Hotel departments whose responsibility particular hotel products are can then be provided with sets of guidelines relating to each department, and these can become *departmental* operational policies.

## Policy Formulation, Communication and Review

The approach described so far to defining the objectives of the hotel and the principles by which it is to be operated as its policies, implies that there are statements expressed in writing, which are laid down from the top, passed down the organization and at least in part also to the outside world, and that these are laid down for all times.

It is, indeed, very desirable that policies should be committed to paper and many hotels do, in fact, express them to a greater or lesser extent in writing and distribute them to those concerned. Leading hotel companies have found that to tell their customers about their policies can be a powerful marketing tool, that personnel policies communicated to staff can have a favourable impact on their image as employers and on personnel relations, that to provide clear policy guidelines for all functional areas and departments to those operating in them is highly conductive to smooth and efficient hotel operation.

The need to communicate formally in writing is to some extent a function of size. It is difficult to do otherwise in a large organization, particularly in one with a number of hotels, which may be dispersed over a wide area. In a smaller organization where there is a high degree of personal contact between the owners, management and employees, and between them and their customers and other parties, and a conscious endeavour in this direction, what the hotel is aiming to achieve and how, can be often passed on informally by word of mouth. But the need to be clear about one's objectives, the need for guidelines and the need to communicate them, remains and is not a function of size.

To define the objectives and the policies is the responsibility of hotel management, but this extends from the directors through managers to heads of departments and supervisors. In all but the smallest hotels and companies there are at least these three levels, all of which are to a varying extent required to contribute to their attainment of the objectives and to the implementation of policies. All three levels can to a varying extent also contribute to the formulation. How much they do so in practice, depends on the style of management. In a strongly authoritarian environment most policy making emanates from the top, with little or no contribution to it from below. In a more participative environment at least those in any position of responsibility can contribute to it. This is not to deny that management is allowed to manage, but a recognition of the fact that there is more than one level of management, that each has a contribution to make according to their respective involvement in the hotel, and that most people carry out policies in whose formulation they participated with greater commitment than those which are just laid down for them.

Objectives and policies change. At any time they should express the best current view of the business and the rules to be adhered to. But as markets, environments in which hotels operate, and most external and internal factors which affect the hotel business change, hotel management have to keep their objectives and policies under review, to meet changing circumstances. New trends in leisure and recreation may provide new opportunities and call for changes in products; new consumer or employment legislation may require changes in the policies of the hotel towards its customers and employees; new sources of supply may suggest changes in purchasing policies and in departmental operational policies. And as policies are adjusted and new ones are formulated, new relationships have to be established with the parties to the hotel business, and management have new guidelines on which to base their decisions in various situations in the conduct of the business.

## Hotel Philosophies

A clear view of the objectives forms a focus for the management of an hotel or a group of hotels; a clear expression of policies establishes a more or less formal frame of reference for decisions in various situations. But in most hotel operations there are also many rules, beliefs and conventions, which are not formulated as policies, and yet they influence how people act, and are accepted by them as part of their everyday conduct of the hotel. They make up what is sometimes referred to as the 'common doctrine' or the 'philosophy' of the business.

Some of the philosophies have to do with ethical standards, which guide management and staff in their dealings with guests, suppliers and others. So, for example, we may believe in being as helpful as possible to those whose bookings we cannot accept when we are full and suggest alternatives; in admitting to our suppliers that we gave a wrong specification when we ordered by telephone; in treating with courtesy the local authority inspector and making his job easier by our cooperation. By contrast we do not discuss disparagingly our competitors with our guests, we do not recruit staff and withhold from them a fact which we know would materially affect their decision to join us or not, and we do not accept gifts from our suppliers.

Our philosophies may be concerned in concrete terms with our operational standards. If we develop a particular concern with and pride in hygiene, impeccable standards of cleanliness in our hotels may become part of everybody's approach to their jobs, and as such part of our philosophy in the conduct of our business, accepted and observed by all our employees.

A philosophy may also express a more general attitude of management. If management has a genuine belief in the contribution employees can make to the conduct of the hotel and in the right to be consulted in matters which affect them, participation in decision-making may become part of our philosophy, adopted more or less automatically in its management and operation.

The philosophy of a business has been well described as 'the way we do things around here'. Some of what comprises the philosophy of an hotel may be regulated by law; philosophy is not made up of legal rules, although to do what is lawful and to avoid what is illegal, may be one of its tenets. There is no sharp dividing line between policies and philosophies. Both are codes dealing with the outlook and approach guiding the hotel in its dealings with others. The former may be more formal and more general, the latter less formal and more specific. And what some hotels may regard as their philosophies, others would refer to as policies.

. . . the Whitbread Group of Hotels has undergone a complete change in the way it has been operated. Areas expected to experience rising demand have been identified as the budget sector with Travel Inn . . . The Travel Inn is the UK's second largest budget hotel group. It is operating in an area where there is high demand and a shortage of supply. In three years' time we plan to operate 100 hotels. This growth will be achieved through further expansion in units operated by our Whitbread franchises - Beefeater and Whitbread Inns as well as the development of new larger Travel Inns at airports and other greenfield sites . . .

The Whitbread Group of Hotels, Strategy for Change 1993/94

## Hotel Plans and Strategies

In pursuing the objectives of the business, hotel management is guided by the policies and philosophies. In order to attain the objectives it is possible just to do one's best, let things happen, and see how it all turns out. A more effective alternative and one more reliably conducive to the attainment of objectives is to plan what is to happen. Planning is developing a constructive concern with tomorrow, deciding what can happen, what should happen and how the desirable is to be accomplished.

*Plans* are, therefore, instruments, which extend the attainable objectives of the hotel in concrete actionable terms for a few months or a year ahead (short-term), for several years (medium-term), for periods longer than a few years (long-term). Plans are normally more numerate instruments than, for example, policies, in that they postulate targets to be achieved, and that they do so as far as possible in measurable terms for given periods of time. Return on invested capital, volume of sales and rates of growth of each, are examples of financial targets; hotel occupancies and rates of labour turnover are examples of physical measurement of attainments in particular areas of the hotel operation.

Plans may be viewed as an expression of the *strategies* of the hotel. In order to meet the needs of particular markets, people and money are the main resources it employs in pursuing its objectives. Decisions have to be made on how to compete in the chosen markets and this extends to the whole of advertising, promotion and public relations (market strategy). In deciding how many people to employ, in what positions, and with what skills, decisions have to be made on how to compete in the labour market (labour strategy). When we determine what sources of capital to use in financing the hotel, how to ensure that the cash flow is adequate and how to contain costs, financial decisions are made regarding profitability (profit strategy). Hotel strategies are, therefore, links between objectives and plans and a means to action-orientated planning in the hotel business.

Hotel entrepreneurs and managers have been often successful in their strategies based on intuitive inspiration rather than systematic exploration, and without systematic planning. But it is legitimate to ask how much more successful they might have been, had they combined their flair with a more systematic approach.

In the long-term an hotel can survive, prosper and meet the aspirations of its owners and employees only through sustained profitability. Its performance cannot be left to chance. Hotel sales, costs and profits have to be charted in advance. Objectives, plans and strategies have to be translated into budgets and *budgetary control* becomes the process to keep the hotel on its course. Operating budgets concerned with income and expenditure are prepared for individual departments and activities and consolidated into a budgeted profit and loss account. Capital budgets concerned with the hotel assets and liabilities are incorporated into a budgeted balance sheet. Continuous comparison of actual and budgeted results showing departures from what was planned enables corrective action to be taken or provides a basis for a revision of what is to be achieved.

It is our aim to be the global market leader by 2000 and we are moving towards this goal with the implementation of a range of new initiatives, resulting from extensive market and customer research. We are determined to generate long-term and consistent competitive product advantage by fully understanding the needs of our target markets – most particularly, the frequent international business traveller.

An important part of our future business strategy will be the development of appropriate non-exclusive partnerships and alliances with a variety of key organisations. This will provide an amplified range of facilities and services designed to meet customer needs more effectively and position our brand more competitively in the market place by enhancing the quality of the travel experience.

We will also continue to develop the company's international position by maximising our coverage of the world's top business centres, establishing new key location hotels by acquiring or developing suitable properties. Moreover, we will continue to focus on local identity – within the chain concept – continuing to make us different from, and more international than, the more uniform chains with which we compete.

Inter-Continental Hotels, Corporate Profile (1993)

However, in practice the planned performance is not confined to financial targets and even these are not necessarily related to individual performance. It is, therefore, necessary to identify those who make key contributions to the performance of the hotel, to evaluate what these contributions are, and to relate targets, both financial and others, closely to individual responsibilities. This approach finds an expression in what is known as *management by objectives* and enables members of the management team to adjust their performance because what is expected of them is based on what they can control and influence, within the totality of the whole hotel. In practice budgetary control and management by objectives are two distinct but interlocking systems.

## The Framework of Hotel Management

It is helpful to see by way of summary how the concepts discussed in this chapter explain the total framework of hotel management. An existing city hotel with its established ways of doing things may have a somewhat different approach from a new resort hotel seeking to establish itself in its market. But both need to be clear about what they are trying to achieve and how to go about it.

There are the objectives – what the hotel is in business to attain. Policies are the rules, on which management bases its decisions in the conduct of the business, and these are supported by the philosophies of the hotel – the less formal rules and conventions. Plans and strategies are the instruments, which direct management towards the attainment of the objectives, with the use of such techniques as budgetary control and management by objectives.

# PART II

Hotel Guest Services

# 4    *Rooms and Beds*

The primary function of an hotel is to accommodate those away from home and sleeping accommodation is the most distinctive hotel product. In most hotels room sales are the largest single source of hotel revenue and in many, more sales are generated by rooms than by all the other services combined. Room sales are invariably also the most profitable source of hotel revenue, which yield the highest profit margins and contribute the main share of the hotel operating profit.

Hotels contributing to annual reports of Horwath International earned on average the proportions of their total revenue shown in Table 3 from room sales in the early 1990s.

**Table 3**
Room Sales as a Ratio of Hotel Revenue in Main Regions

|                              | 1990 (%) | 1991 (%) | 1992 (%) |
| ---------------------------- | -------- | -------- | -------- |
| Africa and the Middle East   | 46.0     | 43.6     | 45.2     |
| Asia and Australia           | 54.1     | 56.0     | 57.9     |
| Europe                       | 49.2     | 49.1     | 47.0     |
| North America                | 63.9     | 62.9     | 71.6     |
| Latin America/Caribbean      | 53.8     | 58.5     | 56.6     |

All figures are arithmetic means.
*Source*: Based on *Worldwide Hotel Industry 1991, 1992, 1993*.

Three main hotel activities are earning the room revenue: hotel reception, uniformed services and housekeeping. Each of them may contribute also to a greater or lesser extent to other hotel activities, but their main functions arise from the requirements of staying guests and they provide the principal hotel services for them.

It is, therefore, convenient to view hotel reception, uniformed services and housekeeping together as components of the hotel accommodation function. In this chapter each is examined in terms of its role in meeting the requirements of hotel guests, their organization and staffing, and accounting and control. This is followed by a similar approach to food and drink and to other hotel services in subsequent chapters.

The three basic components of the accommodation function are present in most hotels and are normally organized in separate departments. But their organization and staffing often differ in hotels of different sizes, types and standards. In smaller hotels only a few people may be engaged in each and cover a wide range of duties; as the hotel increases in size, each activity may be subdivided into separate departments or sections, in which those engaged in them perform more specialized tasks.

A transit city hotel with a short average length of stay calls for a somewhat different approach from that of a resort hotel, which accommodates guests for longer and often such regular periods as one or two weeks. There is also a relationship between prices, the range and quality of facilities and services provided, and the way they are organized. For all these and other reasons it is possible to describe the hotel activities related to the accommodation of guests only in broad and general terms.

## Room Sales

A large proportion of hotel guests reserve their rooms from a few hours to several weeks or months before they actually arrive at the hotel. They do so in person, by telephone, telegram, Telex or Fax, by mail, through travel agents, and in a growing number of cases through central reservations systems. *Hotel reservations* create a multitude of contractual relationships between the hotel and its guests, which begin at the time each reservation is made and continue until the departure of the guests or until their accounts are settled after their stay. Advance reservations are an important responsibility on the part of the hotel, both in the legal and in the business sense, and call for a system which enables room reservations to be converted into room revenue.

When guests arrive in hotels, they are asked to register by providing the receptionist with certain particulars about themselves. The *hotel register*, in which the particulars are entered, has two main functions. One is to satisfy the law, which makes hotel registration of guests a legal requirement in most countries. The second function is to provide an internal record of guests, from which data are obtained for other hotel records.

In most hotels *room allocations* of accommodation reserved in advance are made before the guests' arrival and only guests registering without a previous reservation are allocated rooms on arrival, but in some hotels all room allocations are made only when guests arrive. The registration and room allocation are then the starting point for guests' stay and a signal for the opening of their accounts, as well as for notifying uniformed staff, the housekeeping department, telephonists, and others, of arrivals.

Several *main records* document the room sale in the reception office:

- *reservation form* or *card* standardizes the details of each booking, forms the top sheet of any documents relating to it, and enables a speedy reference to any individual case;
- *reservation diary* or *daily arrival list* records all bookings by date of arrival and shows all arrivals for a particular day at a glance;
- *reservation chart* provides a visual record of all reservations for a period and shows at a glance rooms reserved and those remaining to be sold;
- *hotel register* records all arrivals as they occur and gives details of all current and past guests;
- *reception* or *room status board* shows all rooms by room number and floor and gives the current and projected status of all rooms on a particular day, with details of occupation;
- *guest index* lists all current guests in alphabetical order with their room numbers and provides an additional quick point of reference in larger hotels.

## Mail and Other Guest Services

A combined key and mail rack is a standard feature of most hotel reception offices and reflects two typical responsibilities of the office – room keys and guest mail. Arranged by room number and floor, it corresponds in layout to the reception or room status board and is complementary to it.

In the course of a day's business *room keys* are issued from the rack to arriving guests and to residents who call for them; keys are returned to the rack by guests going out of the hotel or departing at the end of their stay. The rack is a point of reference regarding the occupation of rooms and the whereabouts of guests.

*Mail* may arrive for guests before, during and after their stay at the hotel, and may consist of ordinary or registered mail, packets and parcels, cables and telegrams, Telex messages, Fax transmissions, express mail and personal messages left for guests. Mail awaiting guests' arrival should be handed to them when they are registering; mail arriving after a guest has left the hotel, should be forwarded. During the guest's stay speed is the essence of Fax transmissions, security is the essence of registered mail, bulkiness is the essence of parcels; each calls for standard procedures of their own. But the key and mail rack is the focus; it accommodates much of the mail the guest collects when collecting the room key; it can serve to alert the receptionist to items such as parcels or registered mail, stored elsewhere.

*Three basic aids* are, therefore, related and complementary in the provision of key, mail and other guest services:

● *guest index* shows whether a particular person is resident and that person's room number;
● *reception* or *room status board* shows who is occupying a particular room;
● *key and mail rack* indicates whether the guest is in the hotel and whether there is any mail for that person.

In many hotels the reception office or a separate section of it also acts as *a source of information to guests* – about hotel facilities and services, about the locality, about transport and other matters. In other hotels the keys, mail and information to guests are provided by uniformed staff, and there are usually good reasons for one or the other arrangement. But who does what and to whom the guest can turn, should be made clear to the guest in terms of individual needs and requirements rather than in terms of the hotel organization structure, particularly in larger hotels. Such notices as 'Reception' and 'Hall Porter' have different connotations in different hotels and are not necessarily self-explanatory even for experienced hotel users. Counters and sections of the front hall of the hotel clearly labelled 'Registration', 'Keys', 'Mail', 'Information', 'Guest Accounts', and so on, are more meaningful to guests.

## Uniformed Services

The second component of the accommodation function is uniformed services, which form an integral part of the front hall functions of the hotel and provide a variety of personal services to guests.

*Servicing arrivals and departures* are the most common uniformed services. The meeting and greeting of arriving guests, their luggage and the parking of their cars, are the first responsibilities, which extend from the hotel entrance and car park to the hotel bedrooms. On departure, guests, luggage and transportation are again their primary responsibilities. In an hotel with a hundred departing guests in the morning, followed by a similar volume of arrivals in the afternoon and evening, uniformed staff attend in a day's business to some two hundred people, handle several hundred pieces of luggage, park several dozen cars, and arrange several dozen taxis. The guests, their luggage, and their vehicles, therefore, play a major part in the provision of uniformed services.

During the guest's stay uniformed staff are often the main *source of information* about the hotel and the locality, and the guest's main source of such arrangements as theatre tickets, tours, car hire and other services. The hall porter's desk or an enquiry counter in the front hall are then the information centres of hotels, which contribute much to the range of guest services and to their integration.

In some hotels *other guest services* may be provided by uniformed staff. Newspapers, as well as other small articles, may be supplied to guests by uniformed staff who may also act as messengers, lift operators and men's cloakroom attendants. In many hotels uniformed staff are the only people on duty during the night and particularly in smaller hotels maintain a whole range of hotel services provided by other departments in day time: to receive and register late arrivals, to serve light refreshments, to operate the hotel switchboard, to arrange early morning calls, as well as to clean public rooms and to ensure the security of the hotel.

The provision of uniformed services varies greatly between hotels of different sizes, types and standards, and their organization tends to be influenced by all these factors, as well as by established practices. As mentioned earlier, information to guests may be provided by the reception office or as part of uniformed services or by both. The cleanliness of public rooms may be the responsibility of uniformed staff, the housekeeping department, or outside contractors. What hotel services are available during the night and by whom they are provided, is another source of variation. These differences are legitimate, as long as they reflect the particular requirements of guests and the particular circumstances of each hotel, and as long as the respective functions are defined and understood by staff and made clear to guests where they affect them.

## Hotel Housekeeping

The basic housekeeping function of the hotel is *the servicing of guest rooms*. In its scope, guest bedrooms may be the sole or main responsibility of the hotel housekeeping department, but it may extend to other areas of the hotel.

Normally hotel guests spend at least one-third of their stay in their room. The design, layout, decor, furniture and furnishings of the hotel bedroom are fundamental to meeting their needs and in creating customer satisfaction, and these may be significantly influenced by the housekeeping department. The cleanliness and good order, the linen and other room supplies, and the smooth functioning of the room are the focus of the department. This may include other guest services, such as early morning teas, guest laundry, baby sitting and other personal services. The main housekeeping records are made up of arrival and departure lists and notifications received from the reception office and the housekeeping own room status report, together with separate records in respect of additional services provided by the department.

The *extension of the housekeeping function outside the hotel bedroom* normally includes the cleaning of bedroom floors and may include staircases, public cloakrooms and other public areas of the hotel. However, it is quite common for such public rooms as hotel lounges to be cleaned by uniformed staff, for the responsibility for the men's and women's cloakrooms to be divided between uniformed staff and the housekeeping department, and for restaurants and bars to be cleaned by the staff of those departments. More recently, hotels have been engaging outside contract firms for the cleaning of public rooms.

*Other housekeeping services* often include the provision of first aid to guests and staff, dealing with lost property, and floral arrangements throughout the hotel. When staff accommodation is provided by the hotel, it may be included as part of the head housekeeper's responsibilities. Although in many countries hotels increasingly use outside laundries and dry cleaning firms for their requirements, many hotels operate their own dry cleaning and laundry facilities. These 'in-house' facilities may be then organized as separate departments of the hotel or as sections of the housekeeping department.

This outline of the hotel housekeeping function illustrates three organizational approaches. One seeks to integrate a number of related functions within a major housekeeping department. The second assigns certain functions to the housekeeping department and others to other departments of the hotel, largely on the basis of physical areas. The third consists of 'buying in' certain services from outside suppliers rather than operating them directly as hotel facilities. The considerations involved are discussed further in Chapter 7 as part of the examination of the total hotel organization and also in Chapter 6 in connection with minor operated services.

## Organization and Staffing

The dimensions and characteristics of each hotel are the main determinants of the organization and staffing of the accommodation function. These are discussed further in the context of overall hotel organization in Chapter 7 and hotel staffing in Chapter 8.

Differences in labour intensities between regions and countries are illustrated in tables in this book showing numbers of employees in various hotel activities drawn from annual reports of Horwath International in the early 1990s. To facilitate comparisons, numbers employed are expressed in standardized units of full-time equivalent employees per 100 available rooms.

Hotels in developed countries show lowest numbers employed in major hotel departments, in contrast to hotels in Africa, Asia and Latin America. This applies in particular to housekeeping shown in Table 4; in broad terms twice as many employees are required to service the same number of rooms in some regions compared with others.

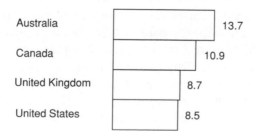

**Figure 4**   Rooms Serviced by Housekeeping Staff, 1992

**Table 4**
Room Employees in Selected Regions and Countries[a]

| | Front desk | | | Housekeeping | | |
|---|---|---|---|---|---|---|
| | *1990* | *1991* | *1992* | *1990* | *1991* | *1992* |
| **Africa and the Middle East** | | | | | | |
| Africa | 9.3 | 9.3 | 11.1 | 15.1 | 25.0 | 21.1 |
| Middle East | 7.9 | 6.9 | 8.4 | 14.4 | 13.9 | 13.8 |
| **Asia and Australia** | | | | | | |
| Asia | 12.0 | 12.6 | 12.3 | 22.8 | 22.7 | 24.3 |
| North Asia | 12.0 | 11.7 | 11.5 | 21.6 | 21.1 | 20.7 |
| Australia | 7.1 | 7.2 | 7.2 | 9.4 | 8.1 | 7.3 |
| **Europe** | | | | | | |
| Continental Europe | 10.1 | 8.4 | 8.5 | 12.3 | 11.1 | 11.1 |
| United Kingdom | 10.3 | 9.8 | 9.3 | 14.1 | 12.5 | 11.5 |
| **North America** | | | | | | |
| Canada | 6.0 | 6.7 | 4.7 | 12.0 | 10.6 | 9.2 |
| United States | 5.7 | 6.3 | 4.6 | 12.2 | 12.9 | 11.7 |
| **Latin America/Caribbean** | | | | | | |
| Mexico | 5.0 | 7.6 | 8.3 | 20.5 | 21.0 | 19.0 |
| South America | 8.4 | 18.3 | 14.2 | 21.2 | 13.4 | 12.7 |
| Caribbean | b | b | 5.4 | b | b | 14.6 |

[a] All figures are medians of numbers of full-time equivalent employees per 100 available rooms.
[b] Included in South America.
*Source*: Based on *Worldwide Hotel Industry 1991, 1992, 1993*.

## Accounting and Control

The financial performance of the hotel accommodation function is reflected in the rooms department operating statement, which shows the revenue and expenses of the department for a given period resulting in the departmental profit. These figures may then be compared with the budget or with the same period of the previous year. Summary illustrations of ratios calculated from operating statements of hotels contributing to Horwath European reports in the early 1990s are shown in Table 5. These indicate significant differences between expenses and profit ratios of hotels in the most developed countries such as the Netherlands, Switzerland and the UK, compared with less developed countries such as Greece, Ireland and Portugal.

**Table 5**
Room Sales, Expenses and Profit Ratios
in Selected European Countries[a]

|  | Room sales[b] (%) | Room expenses[c] (%) | Departmental profit (%) |
|---|---|---|---|
| France | 100.0 | 30.7 | 69.3 |
| Germany | 100.0 | 31.9 | 68.1 |
| Greece | 100.0 | 25.6 | 74.4 |
| Ireland | 100.0 | 26.5 | 73.5 |
| Netherlands | 100.0 | 34.4 | 65.6 |
| Portugal | 100.0 | 27.8 | 72.2 |
| Switzerland | 100.0 | 35.0 | 65.0 |
| United Kingdom | 100.0 | 33.7 | 66.3 |

[a] All figures are arithmetic means.
[b] Revenue from guest accommodation net of any sales or turnover taxes and service charges paid to employees. Revenue from public rooms ordinarily used for food and beverage service is not included.
[c] Rooms payroll including salaries and wages and employee benefits of the personnel of the rooms department plus expenses such as room cleaning supplies, guest supplies, laundry, linen, reservation expenses and travel agents' commissions.
*Source*: Based on *European Hotel Industry 1993*.

These ratios are calculated by most hotels as part of their periodic reporting. On the other hand operating ratios are calculated and monitored more frequently, often daily. There are four key operating ratios and these are illustrated in Table 6.

**Table 6**
Room Occupancies and Average Rates
in Selected European Countries[a]

|  | Room occupancy[b] (%) | No. of guests per room[c] | Average daily rate per room[d] (ECU) | per guest[e] (ECU) |
|---|---|---|---|---|
| France | 64.8 | 1.52 | 150.02 | 100.54 |
| Germany | 63.1 | 1.30 | 82.69 | 65.22 |
| Greece | 71.8 | 1.48 | 37.16 | 25.05 |
| Ireland | 64.1 | 1.63 | 50.53 | 33.81 |
| Netherlands | 64.1 | 1.50 | 77.17 | 51.81 |
| Portugal | 55.3 | 1.48 | 77.45 | 53.61 |
| Switzerland | 60.8 | 1.30 | 117.86 | 96.61 |
| United Kingdom | 57.7 | 1.40 | 63.36 | 50.27 |

[a] All figures are arithmetic means.
[b] Ratio of total occupied rooms to total available rooms.
[c] Average double occupancy calculated by dividing total number of guests by total number of occupied rooms.
[d] Room sales divided by total number of occupied rooms.
[e] Room sales divided by total number of guests.
*Source*: Based on *European Hotel Industry 1993*.

The hotel bedroom will be better designed and become more functional. In appropriate locations the room will have full office facilities both in the form of furniture and available business equipment. The television will provide a wide range of functions, which will include check-out, the provision of basic information, communication both within and outside the hotel, and a wide range of entertainment.

There will be increased emphasis on much improved air purification and ventilation systems. There is already a discernible need for improved lighting in all types of hotel, both in the bedroom and bathroom. The trend towards non-smoking rooms or sections is expected to continue. Better room facilities for the female business traveller will be expected.

Horwath and Horwath, *Hotels of the Future*

# 5    *Food and Drink*

The food and drink service is the second major activity of most
hotels and in many of them it accounts for a larger proportion of
employees than the provision of sleeping accommodation and
related services. This is due to two main factors:

● in contrast to hotel rooms, meals and refreshments in hotels
    may be supplied to non-residents as well as to resident guests
    and include substantial functions sales;
● the provision of meals and refreshments is relatively labour
    intensive.

Hotels contributing to Horwath International annual reports
earned on average the proportions of total revenue shown in Table
7 from food and beverage sales in the early 1990s.

The provision of sleeping accommodation is a service activity, in
which there is a negligible use of materials, and there is no cost of
sales. The provision of meals and refreshments results in composite
products made up of commodities and of service, and the use of
materials represents the cost of sales. Food and drink enter into
meals and refreshments served in hotels in several stages from their
purchase by the hotel to their sale in the same or altered form to
the hotel customer. These processes are described in this chapter as
the food and beverage cycles. According to the size and diversity of
the hotel markets there may be more than one restaurant and bar
and also food and drink service in rooms and through functions.

**Table 7**
Food and Beverage Sales as a Ratio of Hotel Revenue in Main Regions[a]

|  |  | 1990 (%) | | 1991 (%) | | 1992 (%) | |
|---|---|---|---|---|---|---|---|
| **Africa and the Middle East** | Food | 32.0 | | 28.7 | | 31.0 | |
|  | Beverage | 9.6 | 41.6 | 12.1 | 40.8 | 10.9 | 41.9 |
| **Asia and Australia** | Food | 24.9 | | 25.6 | | 23.1 | |
|  | Beverage | 8.8 | 33.7 | 9.1 | 34.7 | 8.4 | 31.5 |
| **Europe** | Food | 30.3 | | 30.1 | | 31.0 | |
|  | Beverage | 13.9 | 44.2 | 14.1 | 44.2 | 14.4 | 45.4 |
| **North America** | Food | 21.7 | | 21.4 | | 17.2 | |
|  | Beverage | 6.1 | 27.8 | 5.8 | 27.2 | 5.2 | 22.4 |
| **Latin America/Caribbean** | Food | 22.6 | | 22.2 | | 21.9 | |
|  | Beverage | 11.4 | 34.0 | 8.0 | 30.2 | 9.9 | 31.8 |

[a] All figures are arithmetic means.
*Source*: Based on *Worldwide Hotel Industry 1991, 1992, 1993.*

The hotel food and beverage operation involves a high degree of technical knowledge and skill, which cannot be dealt with adequately in a book dealing with all aspects of the business. The reader is referred to several texts listed in the further reading for this chapter and in the bibliography.

## The Food Cycle

The food operation of an hotel may be viewed as a cycle, which consists of several stages – purchasing, receiving, storing and issuing, preparing and selling. The stages represent a clear sequence, through which food passes through the hotel from the supplier to the customer.

*Purchasing* is the beginning of the hotel food cycle. Normally one person has a designated responsibility for food purchases – a purchasing officer in a large hotel, the food and beverage manager or one of the assistant managers in a medium-sized hotel; in the smaller hotel purchasing may be undertaken by the owner/manager or the chef, or divided between them as to non-perishable and perishable foods.

The purchasing function extends from identifying best sources of supply, making arrangements with suppliers and placing orders, to close liaison with the kitchen and other user departments regarding requirements, yield and quality, and with the accounts department regarding payment. For foods bought in large enough quantities, purchasing is greatly facilitated by standard purchase specifications, which define quality, size and other features of the required items.

*Receiving* entails ensuring that the hotel is being supplied with food of the ordered quantity and quality at the agreed price, and its transfer to stores or directly to the user departments. Receiving takes place by a comparison of delivery notes against orders and by a physical inspection of the deliveries.

In large hotels there is often a receiving clerk; otherwise receiving may be the responsibility of the storeman; in smaller hotels it may be undertaken by the chef as the principal user.

*Storing and issuing* consists of maintaining an adequate stock of food for the day-to-day requirements of the hotel, without loss through spoilage and pilferage and without capital being tied up unnecessarily through overstocking, and of issues of food to user departments. According to the size of the hotel and its requirements, food stores may be sub-divided, and there may be one or more storemen responsible for them.

Issues to the kitchen and other user departments are normally made at set times in the day against authorized requisitions. Periodical stock-taking takes place to ascertain the value of stocks held in order to determine the food costs for a given period and stock values for accounts purposes.

*Preparing* or food production represents the conversion of the purchased foods by chefs and cooks into dishes and meals, and there are four main aspects in this process:

- volume forecasting seeks to predict the number of meals and of particular items of the menu to be served in each outlet of the hotel each day;
- yields postulate the quantity obtained from items of food after their preparation and cooking;
- recipes give the formulae for producing particular dishes, including the quantities and qualities of ingredients and the method of preparation used;
- portions represent the size or weight of food served to customers.

These four aspects determine the hotel purchasing and operational requirements. Standard yields, standard recipes and standard portions can contribute to effective food cost control through budgeted costs for all menu items.

*Selling* is the final stage of the hotel food cycle and consists of the service of particular foods, dishes and meals by various categories of food service staff to the customer in a restaurant or another hotel facility at particular prices. The main aspects of the selling stage are, therefore, the menu, the form of service and the physical environment and atmosphere in which the sale takes place; these are the three elements of the product, which are reflected in the price.

The menu is the focus of the food operation and there are two main types:

- *table d'hôte* menu is a limited choice menu with a single price for any combination of items chosen or with a price determined by the choice of the main dish;
- *à la carte* menu provides a choice of items, each of which is priced separately.

Three basic levels of service, with variations in each, may be identified as:

- *self-service*, where the customer orders and collects the food from a counter and takes it to a table where he or she consumes it;
- *counter service*, where the customer is presented with the food he or she has ordered and consumes it at the counter;
- *table service*, where the customer is served by a waiter or waitress who takes the order and serves the meal at the table.

The main aspects which make up the physical environment and atmosphere of the hotel eating facility are: the shape and size of the room; the design and decor; the type and layout of seating; the lighting, temperature, noise level, cleanliness and comfort; the age, appearance, and dress of the staff and of guests.

In practice, the selling stage is the starting point in the planning and implementation of the hotel food operation because the type of customer and his requirements determine the most appropriate type of outlet in terms of menu, service, environment and atmosphere, and price. This in turn determines the most desirable type of production, storage and purchasing arrangements.

## The Beverage Cycle

Beverages normally include spirits, wines, beers and minerals, but often exclude other soft drinks which are then treated in hotels as food. The beverage function may be also viewed in terms of a cycle, which represents a sequence through which drink passes from the supplier to the customer.

In comparison with food, it is for a number of reasons a simpler cycle. Many beverages are *purchased* in standard measures under brand names from one or a few suppliers. Although the money value of individual items may be high, by and large, beverages are not perishable, and can be handled in the same form in which they have been purchased through the different stages of the beverage cycle from purchase to sales.

*Receiving* is concerned with ensuring that what is delivered has been ordered and vice versa, but because of the form in which beverages are supplied, it is a relatively simple procedure.

In contrast to food, all beverages are normally *stored* before they are distributed to the selling outlets within the hotel. Although some wines may call for different storage conditions than other wines and other beverages, generally beverages have less specific storage requirements than food, but the need to avoid tying up capital in unnecessary stock applies equally if not more so. Because of the relatively high value of some beverages, frequent stocktaking assumes particular importance.

Whereas food preparation and service are usually separate, each beverage-selling outlet in an hotel combines *preparation and sales* of beverages, and there is normally a standard unit of sale for each. The only variations are likely to occur with cocktails and other mixed drinks.

For all the above reasons *beverage control* is a simpler matter than food cost control and takes one of two basic forms:

● standard gross profit percentages are applied to minerals, beers, wines and spirits, which are then controlled against these standards;
● beverages are issued to selling outlets at selling prices, and controlled against sales.

With these methods each sales outlet is best treated as a separate cost centre, which can be monitored by adjusting issues for changes in stock levels, and this is normally done on a weekly basis.

## Hotel Restaurants

Each hotel normally has one or more restaurants to serve meals and refreshment to resident guests and usually also to non-residents. The number and type of restaurants is determined by the size and diversity of the markets served by the hotel.

One 'multi-purpose' restaurant has to satisfy the needs of most smaller hotel operations with limited non-resident markets for lunch and dinner service. The restaurant then tends to offer a table d'hôte menu or combination of table d'hôte and à la carte menus with waiter or waitress service for main meals, drink is usually available with food, and both are served in a semi-formal environment and atmosphere.

When the market is large enough, the need arises to differentiate first between those seeking full meals who have enough time available to consume them, and those requiring light meals and snacks who have limited time and perhaps also limited means. This differentiation may be introduced by a combination of table and counter service in the same room or through a separation of the two markets between two facilities – a more or less formal restaurant with a broadly based menu open at particular times and an informal coffee shop facility with a limited menu open more or less continuously. The two facilities then offer a choice of differentiated products to different people or to the same people on different occasions. A similar need may be met by a limited service of food in the bar, which is then complementary to the full food service in the restaurant.

A further differentiation may take place in a large hotel with several restaurants with different menus, service, environment and atmosphere. One or more speciality restaurants, including perhaps a nationality restaurant, a restaurant designed to appeal to businessmen, and one to those seeking leisurely dining with entertainment, may comprise the total repertoire of the hotel food service.

Where several restaurants are available in an hotel, it is important to view them as a totality of the hotel food service from the customer as well as from the hotel point of view. They are seen by the customer as a spectrum of facilities, from which choice is made according to who the customer is, and according to the circumstances in which he finds himself at a particular time. For the hotel the individual restaurants represent more or less differentiated products designed to meet particular customer needs, and they are, therefore, complementary in the total food service function of the hotel. The spectrum of customer choice and of hotel product differentiation is expressed through the food, service, environment and atmosphere of each restaurant, through their availability at particular times, and through the prices charged in each.

# Hotel Bars

The size and diversity of the hotel markets are reflected also in the number and type of hotel bars, the main hotel outlets for the service of drinks. In a small hotel one bar may serve residents and non-residents, those having just a drink and those who have a drink before a meal; the same bar may also supply drink to the restaurant and for functions; food may be served in the bar in addition to drink. In larger hotels there may be a residents' bar perhaps combined with television lounge, a lounge or cocktail or a restaurant bar, and one or more separate bars serving functions.

Corresponding to the different types of bar are the three elements of the product – the range of drink available, the form of service, and the environment and atmosphere, with many possible variations in each. But what has been said about hotel restaurants, applies also to hotel bars; where there is more than one outlet, they represent a spectrum of choice for the customer and a range of differentiated products from the point of view of the hotel, which are complementary parts of the total beverage function of the hotel.

# Room Service

In many hotels the guest has a choice of having a breakfast and often also other meals and drinks served in his room, by the same staff who serve in the restaurants and bars, or by the housekeeping staff, or by room (floor) service staff in a large hotel.

When meals and drinks are supplied to rooms as part of the restaurant and bar service, they can be regarded as extensions of the operations of those departments. But in large hotels room service may be organized as a separate department, particularly when it operates from separate floor kitchens. Room service of drinks may be also provided by means of bar units in guest rooms, which are stocked with a selection of alcoholic and non-alcoholic drinks for the use of guests who are charged for the drinks consumed.

Room service in hotels may be seen in two ways. For the guest it is an additional hotel service for his convenience. For the hotel it is an additional product, which may relieve pressures in the restaurant and bars, and particularly through pre-ordered breakfasts and through room bar units it may contribute to a more efficient food and beverage service.

## Functions

Banquets, conferences and similar hotel services may be conveniently grouped together as distinct and separate hotel products under the heading of functions. Their users may also require sleeping accommodation and other hotel services, but several aspects distinguish functions from other parts of the food and beverage operation of the hotel:

● the customers are organized groups such as clubs, societies and other oganizations;
● the organized groups make arrangements for dates and times, numbers attending, menus and other requirements for each occasion, in advance;
● each occasion can be treated as a separate operation planned and organized as such;
● normally the same agreed menu is served to all participants;
● the operation usually takes place in separate rooms and is served by staff who are distinct from those serving others in restaurants and bars, although they may be interchangeable between these facilities.

In smaller hotels functions may be an extension of the activities of the restaurant and bar and the same departments may be responsible for their execution, although the arrangements are usually made with the organizers by the management and in the larger hotels by the food and beverage manager. In hotels with a large volume of functions there is usually a separate banqueting or functions department.

Procedures analogous to advance reservations of bedrooms are then introduced to plan and coordinate this activity of the hotel and the main records include:

● a function agreement, which summarizes the arrangements for each function;
● a function diary, which lists details of all functions in date order;
● a functions chart, which provides a visual record of all functions arranged for a period ahead;

these are supplemented by in-house information and instruction lists, which are distributed to all concerned in the hotel.

Because each function is a separate occasion, with its own price, menu and staffing, it can be closely controlled, especially when food production takes place in a separate kitchen and when the function is provided with its own bar. The revenue and the direct costs can be ascertained with accuracy. Moreover, the volume of identical meals prepared and served together enables higher profit margins to be achieved from functions than from other food and beverage activities, and functions often represent the second most profitable hotel product, after rooms.

## Food and Beverage Support Services

Two main 'back-of-the-house' facilities serve the hotel food and beverage sales facilities – restaurants, bars, room service and functions: the kitchen and the stores.

A major distinction in kitchen facilities in hotels arises from the extent to which they are centralized and serve all the food outlets of the hotel where there is more than one, or whether separate kitchens are provided to serve each restaurant and possibly also room service and functions. The scale and diversity of the food operations are usually the main determining factors but much depends also on the operating preferences and philosophies of hotel managements.

One central kitchen makes for ease of supervision of food production and may also lead to high utilization of equipment and staff. But where meals are produced for several outlets, it may become more difficult to separate the costs of food production attributable to each and conflicts may arise in the priorities demanded by, say, one or more functions taking place when the restaurants may also be at peak pressure.

In large hotels such facilities as baking, butchery and vegetable preparation may be centralized and supply individual kitchens with prepared or partially prepared foods. Alternatively or within the same operation, individual kitchens serving particular outlets may be supplied from a central kitchen, and take the form of 'finishing' kitchens, particularly for outlying function rooms and for room service.

The technical considerations of various food production arrangements, their organization and methods are outside the scope of this book. The reader is advised to consult the numerous texts which deal with the subject, several of which are listed in the suggested further reading for this chapter.

Food and beverage stores in hotels are of three basic types:

- food stores, usually sub-divided into dry stores, perishable stores, cold rooms and in other ways;
- beverage stores or 'cellar';
- linen, china, glass and silver stores.

But storage arrangements in hotels vary. In some hotels the dry stores are the general stores of the hotel, in which are kept not only non-perishable foods, but also cleaning materials, stationery and guest supplies, and the cellar is often used for storing not only minerals, beers, wines and spirits, but also cigars, cigarettes and tobacco. Sometimes the cellar is confined to wines, which call for special storage conditions, and other drink is stored separately in the dry stores. Restaurant linen may be stored in the housekeeping department or in the user departments with china, glass and silver.

## Organization and Staffing

Table 8 shows the numbers employed in food and drink facilities in hotels in various regions and countries drawn from annual reports of Horwath International in the early 1990s.

**Table 8**
Food and Beverage Employees in Selected Regions and Countries[a]

|  | 1990 | 1991 | 1992 |
|---|---|---|---|
| **Africa and the Middle East** |  |  |  |
| Africa | 52.7 | 65.6 | 55.6 |
| Middle East | 47.1 | 30.6 | 36.7 |
| **Asia and Australia** |  |  |  |
| Asia | 55.3 | 52.6 | 57.0 |
| North Asia | 51.9 | 44.0 | 40.6 |
| Australia | 23.1 | 20.2 | 19.3 |
| **Europe** |  |  |  |
| Continental Europe | 34.5 | 29.6 | 28.6 |
| United Kingdom | 42.3 | 32.1 | 31.3 |
| **North America** |  |  |  |
| Canada | 22.3 | 21.3 | 17.2 |
| United States | 21.7 | 27.5 | 21.2 |
| **Latin America/Caribbean** |  |  |  |
| Mexico | 42.8 | 42.6 | 45.2 |
| South America | 38.2 | 26.8 | 18.9 |
| Caribbean | b | b | 24.2 |

[a] All figures are medians of numbers of full-time equivalent employees per 100 available rooms.
[b] Included in South America.
*Source*: Based on *Worldwide Hotel Industry 1991, 1992, 1993*.

As for rooms shown in Table 4, there is a major difference in labour intensities between developed and developing countries. But there are also differences in the incidence of hotels with limited facilities, which is particularly high in North America.

## Accounting and Control

The financial performance of the food and drink facilities in hotels is reflected in the food and beverage department operating statement, which shows the sales and expenses resulting in the departmental profit. An illustration of ratios from operating statements of hotels contributing to Horwath European reports is shown in Table 9. No particular pattern emerges but it is clear that food and drink facilities are barely profitable in French and Portuguese hotels where they make little contribution to overall hotel profitability (Figure 5).

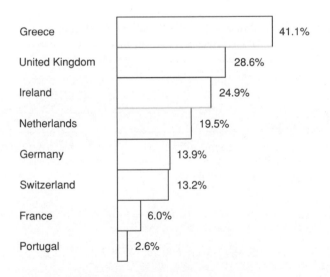

**Figure 5**  Food and Beverage Ratios in European Hotels, 1992

As distinct from financial ratios, the main operating ratios used in food and beverage control are daily seat turnover or rate of seat occupancy, average sales per seat or per customer, and similar measures of utilization and output, which are calculated in a similar way as occupancy and rate statistics described in connection with rooms in the last chapter.

**Table 9**
Food and Beverage Sales, Expenses and Profit Ratios
in Selected European Countries[a]

|  | Sales[b] (%) | Expenses[c] (%) | Profit (%) |
|---|---|---|---|
| France | 100.0 | 94.0 | 6.0 |
| Germany | 100.0 | 86.1 | 13.9 |
| Greece | 100.0 | 58.9 | 41.1 |
| Ireland | 100.0 | 75.1 | 24.9 |
| Netherlands | 100.0 | 80.5 | 19.5 |
| Portugal | 100.0 | 97.4 | 2.6 |
| Switzerland | 100.0 | 86.8 | 13.2 |
| United Kingdom | 100.0 | 71.4 | 28.6 |

[a] All figures are arithmetic means.
[b] Revenue from the sale of food, alcoholic liquor and soft drinks *plus* income from such sources as meeting room rentals and cover charges.
[c] Cost of food and drink *plus* food and beverage payroll including salaries and wages and employee benefits *plus* such items as china, glassware and silver, uniform, cleaning supplies, decorations, guest supplies, laundry, linen, music and entertainment, menu and beverage lists.
*Source*: Based on *European Hotel Industry 1993*.

There is a discernible trend towards more leisure eating in most developed countries. This implies that hotel restaurants will become more specialised, often offering special themes, and many may seek specific market niches.

Competition will arise, not only from conventional restaurants in the vicinity, but from specialised themed restaurants which will often be branded with a high profile, from stores offering high quality prepared take-away foods, and from home catering.

We anticipate that franchising will spread to the hotel restaurant with either the hotel becoming the franchisee or with the restaurant being let to a franchisee. Whether franchised or not, the hotel restaurant may well become a branded product.

Technological advancements will make it possible for even relatively modest hotel restaurants to provide high quality cuisine.

Improved levels of sanitation and hygiene will be expected in both the restaurant and the kitchen.

Horwath and Horwath, *Hotels of the Future*

# *Miscellaneous Guest Services*

Accommodation, food and drink services are the major activities of hotels, which generate all or most hotel revenue, account for all or most of their employees, and represent the principal products provided by the major hotel departments.

But the present-day hotel guest normally also expects other facilities and services. In addition to a comfortable room, and meals and refreshments in a restaurant or bar or in the room, a guest may want to use the telephone or have clothes laundered or dry cleaned. In a large modern hotel a guest may anticipate to be able to buy newspapers, magazines and souvenirs, have a haircut, obtain theatre tickets, and book an airline ticket for the next stage of a trip.

The hotel services other than accommodation, food and drink may be provided to the guest by the hotel or by other operators on the hotel premises. The revenue-earning activities provided directly by the hotel are variously described as ancillary or subsidiary revenue-earning, and are grouped for accounting and control purposes in what are known as minor operated departments, to distinguish them from major operated departments concerned with rooms, food and beverages. Both are distinguished from rental and concession arrangements, under which some of these and other services may be provided to guests by outside firms operating in the hotel.

Several of these services were referred to in Chapter 4 in connection with the hotel accommodation function, as they are often provided by hotel reception, uniformed staff or the housekeeping department. In this chapter they are described as separate sources of hotel revenue with their own organizational and operating considerations.

Hotels contributing to annual reports of Horwath International earned on average the proportions of their total revenue shown in Table 10 from sources other than accommodation, food and drink in the early 1990s.

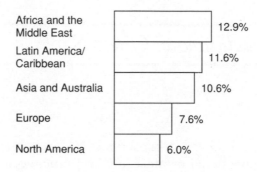

**Figure 6**  Miscellaneous Sales and Income in Hotels, 1992

**Table 10**
Miscellaneous Sales and Income as a Ratio of Hotel Revenue in Main Regions

|  | 1990 (%) | | 1991 (%) | | 1992 (%) | |
| --- | --- | --- | --- | --- | --- | --- |
| **Africa and the Middle East** | | | | | | |
| Telephone | 5.6 | | 6.8 | | 6.6 | |
| Other MOD | 3.3 | | 3.1 | | 3.0 | |
| R and OI | 3.5 | 12.4 | 5.7 | 15.6 | 3.3 | 12.9 |
| **Asia and Australia** | | | | | | |
| Telephone | 3.5 | | 3.0 | | 3.8 | |
| Other MOD | 3.9 | | 3.3 | | 3.1 | |
| R and OI | 4.0 | 11.4 | 3.0 | 9.3 | 3.7 | 10.6 |
| **Europe** | | | | | | |
| Telephone | 2.6 | | 2.8 | | 2.4 | |
| Other MOD | 2.3 | | 2.8 | | 3.0 | |
| R and OI | 1.4 | 6.3 | 1.1 | 6.7 | 2.2 | 7.6 |
| **North America** | | | | | | |
| Telephone | 2.0 | | 2.1 | | 2.6 | |
| Other MOD | 4.2 | | 5.4 | | 1.8 | |
| R and OI | 2.0 | 8.2 | 2.4 | 9.9 | 1.6 | 6.0 |
| **Latin America/Caribbean** | | | | | | |
| Telephone | 4.6 | | 4.6 | | 4.2 | |
| Other MOD | 2.7 | | 2.1 | | 2.5 | |
| R and OI | 4.6 | 11.9 | 4.6 | 11.3 | 4.9 | 11.6 |

All figures are arithmetic means.
Other MOD, other minor operated departments; R and OI, rentals and other income.
*Source*: Based on *Worldwide Hotel Industry 1991, 1992, 1993*.

# Guest Telephones

One of the basic requirements of hotel guests is to communicate with the outside world, and telephone services, which include telegrams, and sometimes also Telex and Fax, are the most common ancillary services provided by hotels for their guests.

A basic provision is telephones with coin boxes, which are available in public rooms for use by resident guests as well as by non-residents. However, this provision is commonly enhanced by bedroom telephones and there are two main operating methods. One is for all calls to be made through the hotel operator who can ascertain the cost of all outgoing calls with the aid of a meter connected to the main switchboard. The other method enables guests to dial calls from their rooms directly, which are recorded by individual meters for each room at the cashier's desk so that charges to guest accounts can be computed from meter readings. The hotel telephone room also often provides telegraph, Telex and Fax services for guests.

Although the same facilities are also used by the hotel for its own communication purposes, there are clearly costs attributable to guest use. There are fixed costs of the premises, semi-fixed costs of equipment rentals and staffing, and variable costs of individual calls and messages through the external system. Incoming calls and messages are normally available to guests free, but most hotels seek to recover not only the variable costs of outgoing calls and Telex and Fax messages, but also some or all of the other costs by a mark-up in the prices charged to guests.

The telephone and related services, therefore, have their own revenue and also their own cost of sales, payroll and other direct as well as indirect costs. In smaller hotels guests may be charged only with the basic cost of their telephone calls and other costs may be regarded as part of the room cost. But hotel telephone and related services are regarded by most larger hotels as a revenue-earning activity and as a cost centre, for which the operating result may be periodically computed in the same way as for other activities of the hotel. If the switchboard operator has also other duties, the payroll cost can be apportioned between the departments concerned and similarly an apportionment can be made for all costs between the guest use and the hotel use of the service.

Clear policies for this service are desirable. In much the same way as a guest may sometimes make doubtful comparisons between the price of a meal in the hotel restaurant and the cost of its ingredients if the meal were cooked at home, comparisons are made by hotel guests between what they are charged for their telephone calls in hotels and what it would have cost them from their own home or office. It is, therefore, important that hotels should take steps to explain the basis of their telephone charges to guests.

## Guest Laundry

Although the increased use of drip-dry clothing has made many hotel guests less reliant on these services, some guests particularly those staying in hotels more than a few days and short-term guests away from home for any length of time often require laundry and valet services in hotels.

These guest services are organized in one of three main ways – as an 'in-house' facility, or by arrangement with an outside laundry and dry cleaning firm or, in an hotel group, laundry and valeting may be operated as a central facility for its hotels. The same facilities may also be used by the hotel for its own purposes – for bedroom and table linen and for the many other fabrics used throughout the hotel.

Whichever of the three arrangements applies, the hotel linen room is usually the focal point of the service. Articles are collected from guests and recorded there before dispatch to the laundry, and returned from there to guests when they have been washed and cleaned – in many hotels as a same-day service.

Although the same facility may be used by guests and by the hotel, each has its own revenue and its own costs. The costs of room linen are part of the room cost and the costs of table linen are part of the restaurant cost; they are included in the room and meal price respectively. The costs of the guests' own laundry and dry cleaning are recovered through a separate charge to the guests' accounts and this normally includes a mark-up on the price charged to the hotel, as a handling charge if an outside firm is used, or as a profit margin to the hotel laundry. For a group laundry it has to be decided whether the profit element accrues to the laundry or to the hotels or whether it is shared by the two.

Guest laundry and valeting are regarded by some hotels as a service to their guests, which is required no more than to cover its direct costs, but in most larger hotels they are treated as a revenue-earning activity, for which revenue and costs are monitored, and for which operating results are computed separately. The hotel incurs costs in providing the service and it seems preferable that these costs are met by those using the service, rather than through higher prices charged to all guests for their stay.

Telephones and laundry have been dealt with here as the two most common ancillary activities in many hotels. Other facilities and services operated by hotels tend to vary greatly from one hotel to another, both in the extent to which they are provided and in the operating arrangements, and are not, therefore, discussed separately in this chapter.

Numbers employed in telephone and other minor operated departments in hotels contributing to Horwath International annual reports in the early 1990s are shown in Table 11. Whilst Table 10 indicates that these activities are more important sources of hotel revenue in less developed regions than in Europe and North America, Table 11 suggests that a similar difference exists when it comes to employment.

**Table 11**
Employees in Minor Operated Departments (MOD)
in Selected Regions and Countries[a]

|  | *Telephone* | | | *Other MOD* | | |
|---|---|---|---|---|---|---|
|  | *1990* | *1991* | *1992* | *1990* | *1991* | *1992* |
| **Africa and the Middle East** | | | | | | |
| Africa | 2.4 | 2.5 | 2.6 | 4.6 | 5.7 | 4.4 |
| Middle East | 2.0 | 2.0 | 1.9 | 4.1 | 5.9 | 8.1 |
| **Asia and Australia** | | | | | | |
| Asia | 2.4 | 2.2 | 2.3 | 7.2 | 5.6 | 6.8 |
| North Asia | 2.1 | 2.0 | 1.9 | 7.3 | 5.6 | 5.0 |
| Australia | 1.3 | 1.0 | 1.2 | 3.0 | 2.3 | 2.7 |
| **Europe** | | | | | | |
| Continental Europe | 1.4 | 1.4 | 1.3 | 3.6 | 3.1 | 3.0 |
| United Kingdom | 2.0 | 1.6 | 1.4 | 5.1 | 3.7 | 3.3 |
| **North America** | | | | | | |
| Canada | 1.0 | 1.0 | 0.9 | 1.6 | 1.3 | n.a. |
| United States | 1.3 | 1.3 | 1.0 | 3.2 | 5.1 | 1.4 |
| **Latin America/Caribbean** | | | | | | |
| Mexico | 2.2 | 1.9 | 2.1 | 5.3 | 4.9 | 4.9 |
| South America | 2.3 | 2.8 | 2.5 | 8.3 | 6.6 | 5.4 |
| Caribbean | [b] | [b] | 2.0 | [b] | [b] | 4.3 |

[a] All figures are medians of numbers of full-time equivalent employees per 100 available rooms.
[b] Included in South America.
*Source*: Based on *Worldwide Hotel Industry 1991, 1992, 1993*.

## Rentals and Concessions

In addition to the hotel trading activities discussed so far, a part of the hotel income may arise from those operated on the hotel premises by others as tenants or concessionaires. The activities carried on by these other operators may or may not be providing a service to hotel guests, but their distinctive feature is that they are not trading activities of the hotel, which sub-lets parts of the premises, thus distinguishing them from the hotel-operated activities. The tenants are in respect of these activities in business on their own account and pay a rent to the hotel.

This type of income arises most commonly from flats and apartments let to tenants for residential purposes on a long-term basis; offices let to business and other organizations for their purposes; shops let to retailers; club rooms let for purposes of a members' or proprietary club; display rooms and show cases let to others for the display of their wares. From the point of view of providing services to hotel guests, the most important in the present context are various retailing activities.

Hotel services to guests may also be provided by concessionaires who are given the right to operate on hotel premises with a view to undertaking services to guests, which would be otherwise operated by the hotel. These may include some of those which may be provided by tenants, such as newsagents, hairdressers and souvenir shops, or other services, such as cloakrooms.

The distinction between direct operation and through rentals and concessions may not be apparent to guests, and in any case may not be material to them, but it is obviously of some significance operationally. There is also a technical legal distinction between rentals and concessions, the former denoting greater independence for the tenant than the licence to use the premises on certain conditions, which is the essence of a concession.

Some types of rental have as their main reason earning income from space which is not required by the hotel for other purposes, or which can earn higher income in that way than it would in another use. In the present context rentals and concessions are seen as alternative means of providing services to guests. Direct management of these services by the hotel normally provides a closer direct control and supervision by the hotel and greater flexibility in operation. However, rentals and concessions relieve the hotel from operating what is often to the hotel operator an unfamiliar service, which enables the hotel to concentrate on its primary activities. In recent years there has been an extension of this approach even to some primary hotel activities, as for example, when an hotel restaurant is operated by another organization.

> Hoteliers should recognise the importance of sports, health and leisure facilities in widening and supporting the sale of bedroom accommodation, as well as in their contribution to profitability. Although the leisure/health centre may itself not be financially viable, its availability is often needed to improve room occupancy, as well as restaurant/bar utilisation. The market expectation of the quality of these facilities will increase.

Horwath and Horwath, *Hotels of the Future*

## Other Income

There are several other sources of income, which may be conveniently included in this chapter, with a view to providing a comprehensive picture of all hotel income, although they do not necessarily arise from the provision of hotel services to guests.

- Commissions may accrue to the hotel from the providers of car hire and taxi services, theatre and travel agencies, and other suppliers of services to guests, in return for the business generated for them by the hotel.
- Foreign currency and travellers cheques are normally exchanged by hotels for guests at rates more favourable to the hotel than those offered by banks, to safeguard against fluctuations in rates between their encashment by the hotel and their sale by the hotel to the bank, and sometimes also to include a charge for the service rendered.
- Salvage represents revenue derived from the sale by the hotel to dealers of such items as used cooking oil, waste paper and other waste or obsolete materials.
- Interest is earned by hotels on bank deposits and other investment of spare funds.
- Cash discounts are earned by hotels by the payment of creditors' accounts within the discount period, as distinct from trade discounts, which are more properly seen as a deduction from the cost of goods and services bought.

## Accounting and Control

The financial performance of minor operated departments of an hotel is reflected in one or more operating statements, prepared in a similar way as for the major operated departments described in

Chapters 4 and 5, and showing departmental revenue, expenses and departmental profit.

Departmental ratios calculated from operating statements of hotels contributing to Horwath International annual reports in the early 1990s are shown in Table 12; this indicates that telephones were a loss-making service in Canada and that minor operated departments generally contributed little to the hotel operating profit in several regions and countries.

**Table 12**
Ratios of Miscellaneous Sales and Income, Expenses and Profit to Total Hotel Revenue in Selected Regions and Countries[a]

| | Telephone | | | Other MOD[d] | | | R and OI[g] (%) |
|---|---|---|---|---|---|---|---|
| | Sales[b] (%) | Exps[c] (%) | Profit (%) | Sales[e] (%) | Exps[f] (%) | Profit (%) | |
| **Africa and the Middle East** | | | | | | | |
| Africa | 7.0 | 4.5 | 1.3 | 2.0 | 1.0 | 1.2 | 2.6 |
| Middle East | 6.9 | 3.7 | 3.0 | 3.6 | 1.6 | 1.8 | 1.8 |
| **Asia and Australia** | | | | | | | |
| Asia | 4.1 | 3.3 | 1.2 | 2.5 | 1.2 | 1.3 | 3.0 |
| North Asia | 4.0 | 2.9 | 1.1 | 2.9 | 1.7 | 1.1 | 1.6 |
| Australia | 2.6 | 2.2 | 0.3 | 1.8 | 1.4 | 0.7 | 1.4 |
| **Europe** | | | | | | | |
| Continental Europe | 3.0 | 1.9 | 1.0 | 1.9 | 1.1 | 0.6 | 1.2 |
| United Kingdom | 2.1 | 1.2 | 1.0 | 1.9 | 1.1 | 0.4 | 3.0 |
| **North America** | | | | | | | |
| Canada | 2.1 | 2.5 | (0.2) | 1.8 | 1.0 | h | 1.2 |
| United States | 2.3 | 1.5 | 0.8 | 1.7 | 1.4 | 0.4 | 0.9 |
| **Latin America/Caribbean** | | | | | | | |
| Mexico | 3.3 | 2.3 | 1.2 | 1.9 | 0.6 | 0.4 | 3.1 |
| South America | 6.7 | 6.7 | 0.7 | 2.0 | 1.6 | 1.0 | 2.0 |
| Caribbean | 5.8 | 3.6 | 1.6 | 3.7 | 2.1 | 0.6 | 8.9 |

[a] All figures are medians.
[b] Revenue derived from the use of telephone facilities by guests.
[c] Cost of calls, payroll and related employee benefits, expenses including equipment rental.
[d] Other minor operated departments.
[e] Revenue derived from laundry and valet services plus income from casino operations, pool club membership, and operated departments other than rooms, food and beverages and telephone.
[f] Payroll and related employee benefits and other departmental expenses of activities under (e).
[g] Rentals and other income.
[h] Negligible amount.
*Source*: Based on *Worldwide Hotel Industry 1993*.

# PART III

Hotelmen and Methods

# *Hotel Organization*

Organization is the framework in which various activities operate. It is concerned with such matters as the division of tasks within firms and establishments, positions of responsibility and authority, and relationships between them. It introduces such concepts as the span of control (the number of subordinates supervised directly by an individual), levels of management (the number of tiers through which management operates), delegation (the allocation of responsibility and authority to designated individuals in the line of 'command'). This chapter is concerned with characteristics of hotel organization rather than with management concepts.

Until not so long ago – about the middle of this century and even later than that – the typical hotel of almost any size was characterized by a large number of individuals and departments directly responsible to the hotel manager who was closely concerned with his guests and with all or most aspects of the hotel operation. There might have been one or more assistant managers who had little or no authority over such key individuals as the chef, the head waiter or the housekeeper. The hotel manager usually combined the 'mine host' concept of hotel keeping with a close involvement in the operation. He normally had all or most of the technical skills that enter into the business of accommodating and catering for guests. Although he might have given more attention to departments in which he felt confident about his expertise, and less to those in which his knowledge and skills might have been lacking, his approach was essentially that of a technician rather than the manager of a business. Hotels served those who chose to use them. The financial control was exercised by the owners or by accountants on their behalf. Personnel management rarely extended beyond the 'hiring and firing' of staff. Hotel buildings and interiors were not often viewed as business assets required to produce a return comparable to other commercial investments; maintenance and energy were cheap.

Several influences have tended to change this profile generally and the approach to hotel organization in particular in the second half of the twentieth century. The market for hotels, the number of hotels, and the size of individual operations have grown, against the background of economic and social conditions in most parts of the world. Business and management thought and practice have found their way into hotels, with the entry into the hotel business of firms engaged in other industries, development of hotel education and training, and higher quality of management. Innovation in hotel organization, at first largely confined to a few firms in North America, has spread to others in other countries. These and other influences have brought about changes in the ways in which hotels organize their activities today.

Three particular developments illustrate the changes in hotel organization in post-war Britain. One relates to the grouping of functions. In the early 1950s hotel reception, uniformed services and housekeeping were invariably regarded as separate departments, each reporting directly to the hotel manager; twenty years later many large hotels had front hall managers, rooms managers, or assistant managers with specific responsibilities in this area. Similarly, over the same period in most large hotels food and beverage managers came to be appointed, responsible for all the hotel activities previously organized in restaurants, bars and kitchens under the direct control of the hotel manager. Secondly, there has been a growth in specialists. In the early 1950s only a few large hotels had a staff manager, a public relations officer or a buyer; by the early 1970s personnel, sales and marketing, and purchasing departments were common features of the large hotels and of hotel groups. Thirdly, where each hotel used to be more or less self-sufficient in the provision of its various guest services and supporting requirements, many of these are now provided through internal rentals and concessions and through specialist suppliers and operators such as outside bakeries, butcheries and laundries.

Organization is a function of purpose and the complexity of the hotel business arises because it is concerned with several distinct products, services and facilities, which are offered in various combinations, as we saw in Part II of this book. It is helpful to arrange these, and the hotel activities described in Parts III and IV, into a simple framework along the lines of those six chapters, and the classification of activities outlined below follows the common pattern of uniform and standard systems of accounts in use in a number of countries:

| Operated departments (revenue-earning) | Major (primary) | Rooms<br>Food<br>Beverages |
| | Minor (ancillary) | Guest telephones<br>Guest laundry and valeting<br>Other guest services |
| Support service departments (undistributed overhead) | | Administration and general<br>Marketing<br>Property operation, maintenance and energy |

In this schedule a distinction is drawn first between revenue-earning services operated by the hotel (dealt with in Part II of this book) and activities that service the hotel (dealt with in Parts III and IV). The revenue-earning services are divided further into primary and ancillary (dealt with in Chapters 4 and 5 and in Chapter 6 respectively). It has been found in practice that the most effective hotel organization structures follow this classification and provide for clear profit and cost centre responsibilities.

## Rooms

In Chapter 4 the accommodation function of the hotel is described in terms of reception, uniformed services and housekeeping. Several typical organizational approaches may be identified in respect of these activities in practice:

● all three activities operate as separate departments with their own heads of department;

● reception and uniformed services are grouped together as the front hall or front house of the hotel under an assistant manager for whom this is the sole or main responsibility;

● reception and uniformed services are grouped together as a front hall or front house department with its own head of department;*

---

* This approach is illustrated in Figure 7 (p.81).

- all three activities are grouped together as the rooms department under an assistant manager for whom this is the sole or main responsibility;
- all three activities are grouped together as the rooms department with its own head of department.

The first approach provides for a direct line of responsibility and authority between each separate head of department and the hotel manager and hence for a close contact between the two levels of management; however, it extends the hotel manager's span of control and he is required to coordinate the separate departments. The other four approaches are designed to reduce the hotel manager's span of control and provide for a coordination of related activities at an intermediate level, but increase the number of levels through which management has to operate, and reduce the amount of direct contact between the hotel manager and the departments concerned.

Several activities were described in connection with rooms, which may be arranged differently in large hotels:

- In most hotels advance reservations form an integral part of hotel reception and the same employees deal with them and with other reception tasks. But advance reservations may be dealt with in a separate section of the reception office or in a separate department, to enable employees to concentrate on the respective tasks without conflicting demands on their time and attention. Sometimes all advance reservations are concentrated in the sales department, which has a responsibility for maximizing hotel occupancy.
- In smaller hotels guest accounts are normally handled by book-keeper/receptionists, but strictly speaking guest accounts represent an extension of the accounting function of the hotel. Therefore, where guest accounting is handled by bill office clerks and cashiers, they normally form a part of the accounts department.
- In some hotels room service is provided by housekeeping staff, but room service is clearly part of the food and beverage function of the hotel.

## Food and Beverages

In Chapter 5 the food and beverage function of the hotel is described in terms of the food and beverage cycle, the main sales outlets, and the related support services. Several typical organizational approaches may be identified in respect of this function in practice:

    each sales outlet and supporting service operates as a separate department with its own head of department;

    several departments are grouped together under an assistant manager for whom they represent the sole or main responsibility, e.g. purchasing and storage, bars and cellars, the 'back-of-the-house' activities including the kitchen, and so on;

    several of these departments are grouped together as one department under its own head of department;

    all food and beverage activities are grouped together under an assistant manager for whom they represent the sole or main responsibility;

    all food and beverage activities are grouped together as a food and beverage department with its own head of department.*

The same observations apply to these approaches as are made above in relation to rooms, regarding lines of responsibility and authority, span of control and levels of management; the size of the span of control and the number of management levels are conflicting considerations.

Several aspects of the food and beverage function are closely related to each other but also to other parts of the hotel operation:

    Most hotels have facilities serving both food and beverages, although in some of them food or beverages may predominate. Whilst it is usually relatively easy to separate the revenue from each, it is often impractical to separate accurately all the costs of operation other than the cost of sales, because the same employees may handle both products, and because other goods and services provided in the same outlet may not be readily identifiable as either food or beverages. In these circumstances food and beverages are treated together, analysed by sales outlet, and the related responsibilities are reflected in the organization structure.

    Food and beverage control based on the food and beverage cycles described in Chapter 5 may be appropriately seen as part of the total accounting function of the hotel. In these circumstances such employees as restaurant cashiers and cost control clerks are included on the staff of the hotel accountant.

---

* This approach is illustrated in Figure 7 (p. 81).

● Where there is a separate sales department, food and beverage sales are usually closely monitored by that department, and such arrangements as reservations for functions may form part of the responsibilities of the sales department.

## Miscellaneous Guest Services

In Chapter 6 miscellaneous guest services are illustrated in terms of such activities as telephones and laundry and the typical organizational approaches for most of them are shown to be of two main kinds:

● the services are operated under direct management of the hotel as minor operated departments;
● the services are operated under rental and concession arrangements with the hotel by another firm.

The alternative arrangements may apply in the provision of the following main services to guests:

| | |
|---|---|
| beauty shop and hairdressing | secretarial services |
| florist | squash courts and tennis courts |
| garage | gifts and souvenirs |
| laundry and dry cleaning | swimming pool |
| newspapers and magazines | tobacconist |

Direct management of these services normally provides for a closer direct control and supervision by the hotel and for greater flexibility in operation. In many hotels the services are merely grouped as residuary hotel activities for accounting and control purposes and are in practice provided as part of the services of other hotel departments, e.g. reception, uniformed services, housekeeping or general administration, and are not separate departments in the organizational sense. Only when the volume of a particular service is sufficiently large, it may be organized as a separate department. And it is only then that the option arises for the service to be provided for the guests by another operator, because it warrants his involvement, under a rental or concession arrangement. Such arrangement then relieves the hotel from operating what is often to the hotel operator an unfamiliar service and allows it to concentrate on its primary activities.

Therefore, major deciding factors are the size of the operation, the availability of suitable operators of particular services, and the operational philosophies of the hotel or hotel group, as well as the quality of service and the financial return to the hotel, which may result from one or the other approach.

## Hotel Support Services

Earlier in this chapter hotel activities were classified into revenue-earning and support service departments. The first group is considered in Part II of this book, the second in Parts III and IV. The first of the support service departments – administration and general – relates to functions of general management (some of which are considered in this chapter), purchasing (discussed in connection with food and beverages in Chapter 5, although not confined to them), personnel (dealt with in Chapter 8) and accounting and control (included in Chapter 12). The remaining support services are covered in Chapters 10 and 11.

In practice the non-revenue service activities are organized in one of three main ways:

- retained among the hotel manager's own responsibilities;
- assigned to an assistant manager as one of his or her responsibilities;
- assigned to a separate department with its own head of department.

To a greater or lesser extent each of these activities may also draw for its performance on external specialist advice and assistance.

The main specialist activities, which may be organized in one of these ways, and examples of the external sources of advice and assistance available to the hotel in respect of each can be summarized as follows:

Accounting and finance   Hotel accountants and consultants
Public accountants and auditors
Professional stock-takers

Personnel services   Personnel recruitment and selection
specialists

Work study, personnel and industrial
relations advisers
Training boards and other agencies

| Purchasing | Hotel accountants and consultants |
| | Furniture and equipment specialists |
| | Various suppliers |
| | |
| Sales and marketing | Market research agencies |
| | Advertising agencies |
| | Public relations consultants |
| | |
| Property operation, | Architects, builders, designers |
| maintenance, energy | Consulting engineers |
| | Utility undertakings |

Advisory services are also sometimes provided by professional bodies, trade associations for their members, the technical press and other agencies.

Apart from any operational philosophies, the adoption of the organizational approaches, in respect of a particular activity, is largely determined by the size of operation: the first is normally associated with a small hotel; the second with medium size; and the third with large operations, but no hard and fast rules apply. Each of these activities comprise specialist knowledge and skills, as distinct from normal operational know-how inherent in the primary operating activities.

## The Management Structure

Following the discussion of the division and grouping of operated and service activities into departments, it is next necessary to consider the total management structure of the hotel; this comprises all positions of responsibility and authority below top management, which is represented in an hotel company by the board of directors. The management team consists of the hotel manager, one or more deputy or assistant managers, and the heads of departments. A discussion of the management structure is concerned with these posts and with the relationships between them.

According to the size of the hotel and the particular arrangement in operation, the hotel chief executive may be variously designated as managing director, general manager or simply hotel manager. He or she may to a greater or lesser extent participate in the formulation of the hotel policies and strategies, and will invariably be responsible for their implementation and for the hotel performance. In larger hotels this level may be sub-divided between a managing director or general manager and the hotel manager or a resident manager. The former then reports to the board and normally coordinates the work of the specialist departments and of the hotel or resident manager, who is in turn responsible for the day-to-day management of the hotel activities.

The complexity and continuity of the hotel activities normally give rise to the need for one or more deputy or assistant managers. A deputy hotel manager normally has authority over the heads of departments. But there is much variation in the role, authority and responsibilities of hotel assistant managers.

In some instances they are the hotel manager's deputies in all but name, in respect of the whole operation or some parts of it, e.g. food and beverages, front hall, 'back of the house', and so on; in other cases they have these specific responsibilities in addition to their general role as the manager's deputies. But many so-called assistant managers perform roles, which are more appropriately described as those of general assistants (assisting where required throughout the hotel) or of personal assistants to the manager (acting on his behalf as he directs them to do). Yet in other cases their main role is guest contact.

All the roles described above may be appropriate in particular circumstances, but effective hotel management calls for a clear definition of responsibility and authority. The relationships with heads of departments are especially important in this context. Titles, which describe the particular roles, can be helpful in this direction.

In order to provide clear-cut lines of responsibility and authority and an effective coordination of related activities, some hotels function without assistant managers as such: those who would normally be in such positions are allocated specific responsibilities and appropriate titles to describe them.

Those in positions of heads of departments fall into two distinct categories. Heads of operated departments are known as line managers, with direct lines of responsibility and authority to their superiors and to their subordinates in respect of each operated department. Heads of service departments are specialists who provide advice and service to line management, and relieve them of such specialist tasks as are considered to be more effectively discharged through the appointment of specialists; they have no direct authority over employees other than those of their own departments. Line management includes, for example, head receptionists, head housekeepers, head chefs and restaurant managers. Specialists include accountants, buyers, personnel and purchasing officers and similar posts. In order to draw a distinction between the two, it is helpful to confine the designation 'manager' to operated departments.

It is also relevant to refer in this context to a confusion, which often arises with various trainee positions. It is difficult to justify such titles as 'trainee manager' unless its holder has been designated to fill a specific post, for which he is training. A person who is undergoing training with a view to an ultimate unspecified position of responsibility is more appropriately described as a management trainee.

## Organization Structure of a Large Hotel: an Illustration

Some of the concepts discussed in this chapter are illustrated in the organization chart of a large London hotel with several hundred rooms, extensive food and beverage facilities and several hundred employees (Figure 7). In this instance a conscious attempt has been made to introduce a management structure designed to reduce the span of control of those concerned with the coordination of related activities and to provide a high degree of delegation.

Each position in the chart carries specific responsibilities and also overall responsibilities common to all management positions, such as the implementation of policy in relation to sectional requirements, employee motivation, training, safety, adherence to budgets and accountability for the performance and results of the department(s) for which a particular individual is responsible. However, each individual is responsible only for those results they can control.

The organization chart is supported by schedules of management responsibilities, which state for each position the title, the responsibilities of the post, the immediate superior, the relationships with other management positions within the organization, as well as the requirements of the post in terms of age, education, training, experience and any special requirements.

A 'principle of three' has been introduced in this hotel in decision-making. For example, menu planning for each outlet is undertaken by the food and beverage manager, the chef and the appropriate departmental head; full-time members of staff are engaged by the personnel officer, the immediate and the next but one superior of the employee.

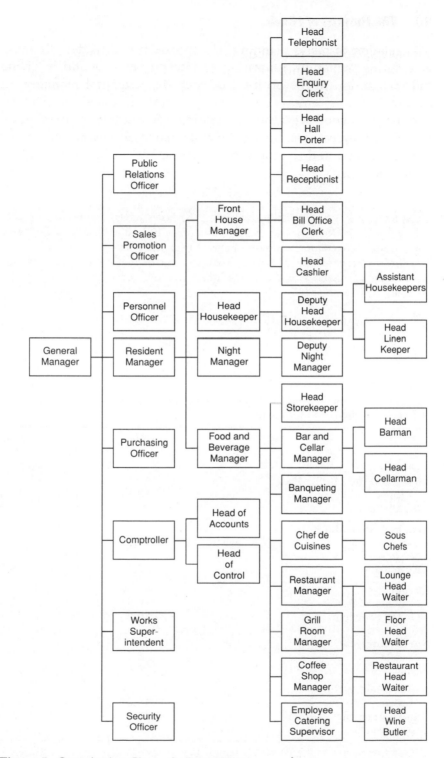

**Figure 7** Organization Chart of a Large Hotel

In relation to menu planning this approach is considered helpful in securing maximum utilization of kitchen facilities and in giving full recognition to the position of each departmental manager. In relation to staff engagement the principle is considered to be conducive to good selection, to creating a favourable impression on future employees, to securing the acceptance of new employees by their superiors, and to establishing a close knowledge of employees by management.

The traditional organisational structure of the hotel needs re-assessment at all sizes and levels. Reporting lines have sometimes been ill-defined and/or over-administered. Accountability has not always been aligned with responsibility.

The whole category of junior management/department head may be becoming obsolete, with a better educated labour force and management utilizing new technology . . .

Horwath and Horwath, *Hotels of the Future*

**Table 13**
Administrative and General Expenses as a Ratio of Hotel Sales in Selected Regions and Countries[a]

|  | 1990 (%) | 1991 (%) | 1992 (%) |
|---|---|---|---|
| **Africa and the Middle East** | | | |
| Africa | 10.3 | 7.1 | 11.4 |
| Middle East | 9.1 | 8.2 | 8.9 |
| **Asia and Australia** | | | |
| Asia | 8.5 | 7.6 | 7.8 |
| North Asia | 7.3 | 8.3 | 8.0 |
| Australia | 7.9 | 9.3 | 8.4 |
| **Europe** | | | |
| Continental Europe | 9.5 | 9.3 | 9.0 |
| United Kingdom | 9.2 | 9.2 | 10.1 |
| **North America** | | | |
| Canada | 8.4 | 8.9 | 10.6 |
| United States | 9.8 | 10.4 | 10.2 |
| **Latin America/Caribbean** | | | |
| Mexico | 15.2 | 16.2 | 17.5 |
| South America | 13.0 | 13.9 | 8.0 |
| Caribbean | b | b | 15.8 |

[a] All figures are medians.
[b] Included in South America.
*Source*: Based on *Worldwide Hotel Industry 1991, 1992, 1993*.

# Accounting and Control

In hotel uniform and standard systems of accounts operational expenses relating to the whole hotel, as distinct from those relating to particular operated departments, are treated as undistributed operating expenses. They are commonly classified in four main groups: administrative and general; marketing; energy; property operation and maintenance.

The first category, administrative and general expenses, covers to a great extent the payroll and other expenses of general management, accounting and control. Their incidence in hotels contributing to Horwath International reports in the early 1990s is shown in Table 13 and in European hotels in Table 14. In most global regions, with the major exception of Latin America and the Caribbean, administrative and general expenses amount to around 8-10 per cent of total sales. Among European countries that level is significantly exceeded only by Ireland.

**Table 14**
Administrative and General Expenses as a Ratio of Hotel Sales
in Selected European Countries[a]

|  | *Payroll and related expenses* | | | *Other expenses* | | |
|---|---|---|---|---|---|---|
|  | *1990* (%) | *1991* (%) | *1992* (%) | *1990* (%) | *1991* (%) | *1992* (%) |
| Austria | 4.1 | 5.2 | n.a. | 3.8 | 6.7 | n.a. |
| France | 5.7 | 5.5 | 6.0 | 3.9 | 3.3 | 5.6 |
| Germany | 3.9 | 4.2 | 4.2 | 3.8 | 3.3 | 4.1 |
| Greece | 7.4 | n.a. | 5.5 | 2.6 | n.a. | 4.5 |
| Ireland | 6.2 | 6.0 | 7.0 | 6.3 | 6.9 | 7.2 |
| Netherlands | 5.5 | 5.3 | 5.3 | 4.6 | 5.3 | 4.6 |
| Portugal | 4.9 | 4.4 | 5.2 | 5.5 | 4.5 | 5.5 |
| Switzerland | 4.5 | 4.7 | 4.3 | 2.8 | 3.1 | 2.8 |
| United Kingdom | 4.2 | 4.6 | 5.8 | 5.2 | 4.9 | 4.8 |

[a] All figures are medians.
*Source*: Based on *European Hotel Industry 1991, 1992, 1993*

The number of employees in these activities per 100 rooms appears in Table 15, which shows major differences between developed and developing regions and countries.

**Table 15**
Administrative and General Employees in Hotels
in Selected Regions and Countries[a]

|                              | 1990 | 1991 | 1992 |
|------------------------------|------|------|------|
| **Africa and the Middle East** |      |      |      |
| Africa                       | 12.8 | 18.1 | 14.4 |
| Middle East                  | 11.4 | 11.1 | 12.3 |
| **Asia and Australia**       |      |      |      |
| Asia                         | 13.6 | 12.5 | 13.7 |
| North Asia                   | 10.9 | 9.6  | 9.3  |
| Australia                    | 7.2  | 5.1  | 4.9  |
| **Europe**                   |      |      |      |
| Continental Europe           | 5.6  | 6.3  | 4.7  |
| United Kingdom               | 8.6  | 7.4  | 8.0  |
| **North America**            |      |      |      |
| Canada                       | 6.0  | 5.3  | 4.7  |
| United States                | 3.8  | 4.3  | 2.3  |
| **Latin America/Caribbean**  |      |      |      |
| Mexico                       | 16.9 | 15.3 | 14.7 |
| South America                | 12.7 | 10.9 | 6.0  |
| Caribbean                    | b    | b    | 15.3 |

a All figures are medians of numbers of full-time equivalent employees per 100 available rooms.
b Included in South America.
*Source*: Based on *Worldwide Hotel Industry 1991, 1992, 1993*.

*Hotel Staffing*

It is difficult to consider any aspect of hotel operations without reference to staffing and it is impossible to confine staffing considerations to a single chapter. Staffing and related aspects of hotel operations, therefore, receive some attention throughout this book. It is helpful to set this chapter in the context of the various references made to staffing earlier and also subsequently, so that a wider view may be taken of the human resources in the hotel business by linking together the separate parts.

In Chapter 1 hotels are seen as important employers of labour, in Chapter 2 the service provided by employees is described as an integral element of hotel products, and in Chapter 3 hotel employees enter into the policies, philosophies and strategies of the business. The organization and staffing of the revenue-earning activities of hotels are considered in Chapters 4–6, and similarly these matters are included in relation to the servicing activities of hotels in Chapters 10–12. Several of these considerations are brought together in Chapter 7 as part of the discussion of hotel organization. Productivity in hotels forms a separate Chapter 9. The distinctive characteristics of small hotels, hotel groups and international hotel operations are outlined in Chapters 13–15.

The concern with human resources of the hotel, or the personnel function, as it is usually described, covers the following main aspects:

- job analysis, manpower planning and scheduling of work;
- recruitment, selection and training of employees;
- job evaluation, conditions of employment and welfare of employees;

- promotion, retirement and termination of employment;
- employee consultation, negotiation and the handling of disputes.

The employment of people in hotels in different countries takes place in particular economic, political and social environments, in hotels with different market and operating conditions, customs and practices; increasingly employment is regulated by laws of those countries. It is, therefore, less than realistic to attempt to deal with the various aspects of the personnel function in a way which would be meaningful to all or most hotels. This chapter has particular and somewhat limited aims and scope, and focuses on three aspects: determinants of hotel staffing, variations in hotel staffing to be found in different regions and countries, and the organization of the personnel function, which may be applicable beyond the boundaries of one country. There are many texts dealing more or less comprehensively with the personnel function, some of them specifically in hotels, and several of those available in Britain are listed as suggested further reading for this chapter.

## Determinants of Hotel Staffing

In their study of British hotels, the Department of Employment Manpower Research Unit identified eight main factors* that determine hotel staffing:

- *Size of hotel* (number of bedrooms, number of beds, number and size of restaurants, etc.) determines the scale and type of operations and the extent to which economies of scale can be achieved. Large hotels tend to have a lower staff/guest ratio than medium-sized hotels and the ratio was also found to be low in smaller owner/managed hotels where the owner and his family generally work longer hours and employ fewer staff.
- *Ownership* may affect staffing by its influence on the scale of operation and through the owner's attitude to hotelkeeping. Group-owned hotels tend to be larger and more standardized than the independent hotels, which tend to be more individualistic.
- *Age and layout of the buildings* affects the efficiency of hotel operations and, therefore, the staffing levels. Modern purpose-built hotels with a view to ease and economy of operation can operate with fewer staff than older hotels, which are more difficult and expensive to operate.

*Manpower Studies No. 10, HMSO, 1971.

● *Range and type of facilities and services* influence the number and type of staff required to provide them. Generally the greater the variety of food and beverage facilities and of other guest services within the hotel, the greater the staffing requirements.

● *Methods by which hotel services are provided* have a pronounced effect on the number and skills required to provide them. Hotel services may be provided personally by staff or through self-service and other non-personal methods with wide variations in required staffing.

● *Quality of staff* has a bearing on their output and, therefore, on the number of staff required to provide a particular volume and standard of hotel facilities and services. This is a matter of attitude, motivation and training.

● *Organization* influences the staffing of hotels through the division of tasks and responsibilities, the extent of use of labour-saving equipment, techniques and procedures, and the extent to which specialist contractors and suppliers are used for particular hotel requirements.

● *Incidence of demand*, annually, weekly and during the day, gives rise to annual, weekly and daily fluctuations in staffing requirements, which can be met to a varying extent by the employment of temporary, casual and part-time staff.

## Hotel Products and Staffing

Table 16 compares numbers employed in various hotel activities in different regions and countries. It suggests wide variations in the staffing of the same activities but in all regions and countries food and beverage employees are the largest single group.

Numbers of employees in different departments depend on several factors, including the relative importance of each activity in the total hotel operation, and also on the criteria used in allocating employees between departments. The data in Table 16 cover mainly large first-class hotels and employees are allocated to departments on the basis of the *Uniform System*.

The distribution of employees between the various activities of the hotel provides a broad indication of the occupational requirements of the hotel operation. Generally even smaller hotels require a range of several quite distinct skills and attributes in their employees, and the larger the hotel, the greater the range and complexity of its staffing.

**Table 16**
Numbers of Employees in Hotel Activities in Selected Regions and Countries[a]

| | Rooms | | Food and | MOD[b] | | Admin. and | Marketing | | | | |
| | Front desk | H'keeping | beverage | Telephone | Other | general | Sales | Other | Property[c] | Other | Total |
|---|---|---|---|---|---|---|---|---|---|---|---|
| **Africa and the Middle East** | | | | | | | | | | | |
| Africa | 11.1 | 21.1 | 55.6 | 2.6 | 4.4 | 14.4 | 2.9 | 0.8 | 11.0 | 17.8 | 147.4 |
| Middle East | 8.4 | 13.8 | 36.7 | 1.9 | 8.1 | 12.3 | 2.4 | n.a. | 10.0 | 7.9 | 92.0 |
| **Asia and Australia** | | | | | | | | | | | |
| Asia | 12.3 | 24.3 | 57.0 | 2.3 | 6.8 | 13.7 | 2.9 | 0.9 | 7.2 | 6.6 | 141.5 |
| North Asia | 11.5 | 20.7 | 40.6 | 1.9 | 5.0 | 9.3 | 2.1 | 0.8 | 5.7 | 5.4 | 94.0 |
| Australia | 7.2 | 7.3 | 19.3 | 1.2 | 2.7 | 4.9 | 1.8 | 0.7 | 2.2 | 3.1 | 45.0 |
| **Europe** | | | | | | | | | | | |
| Continental Europe | 8.5 | 11.1 | 28.6 | 1.3 | 3.0 | 4.7 | 1.6 | 0.9 | 3.0 | 4.5 | 68.4 |
| United Kingdom | 9.3 | 11.5 | 31.3 | 1.4 | 3.3 | 8.0 | 1.9 | 0.8 | 3.5 | 4.2 | 71.4 |
| **North America** | | | | | | | | | | | |
| Canada | 4.7 | 9.2 | 17.2 | 0.9 | n.a. | 4.7 | 2.0 | n.a. | 1.8 | n.a. | 38.6 |
| United States | 4.6 | 11.7 | 21.2 | 1.0 | 1.4 | 2.3 | 1.6 | 0.7 | 2.4 | 3.0 | 48.6 |
| **Latin America/Caribbean** | | | | | | | | | | | |
| Mexico | 8.3 | 19.0 | 45.2 | 2.1 | 4.9 | 14.7 | 2.3 | 0.6 | 12.0 | 6.2 | 112.8 |
| South America | 14.2 | 12.7 | 18.9 | 2.5 | 5.4 | 6.0 | 2.2 | 1.0 | 4.2 | 4.6 | 54.7 |
| Caribbean | 5.4 | 14.6 | 24.2 | 2.0 | 4.3 | 15.3 | 1.9 | 0.8 | 11.7 | 4.2 | 97.2 |

[a] All figures are medians of numbers of full-time equivalent employees per 100 available rooms.
[b] Minor operated departments.
[c] Property operation and maintenance.
*Source:* Based on *Worldwide Hotel Industry 1993.*

The operating conditions of various hotels, the range of skills and occupations, their grouping in departments, and the conditions of work, are some of the distinctive features of employment in hotels. The staffing of hotels has particular requirements and poses particular problems for management, especially when the personnel function is interpreted as dealing with more than just the process of employment. It is, therefore, important to consider how the personnel function may be organized.

## Organization of the Personnel Function

The various aspects of the personnel function may be the direct responsibility of the hotel manager in a smaller hotel, but as the size of the operation increases, the manager may delegate some or all of them to an assistant manager. In a large hotel or in an hotel group the personnel function is normally the responsibility of a separate personnel department, which forms one of the main service departments of the hotel. In any hotel where the responsibility is delegated, line management is to a greater or lesser extent concerned with aspects of the personnel function too. Whilst personnel administration – the various employment procedures in particular – may be removed from line managers, they nevertheless normally participate in employee selection and usually also in on-the-job training; through the direction and supervision of employees they are also directly concerned with the human relations of the business generally.

The particular responsibilities involved and how they may be organized, can be seen most clearly in hotel operations where they are highly developed and specialized. This is illustrated in what follows in the example of an hotel group, which operates eighteen London hotels with some 3500 employees. The illustration of the organization of the whole personnel function is followed by an illustration of the approach of the same company to training, one of the integral component functions of the personnel department.

The organization of the central personnel department and the relationship between the centre and individual hotels is summarized in outline in Figure 8 and in Table 17. This is not necessarily typical of the approaches adopted in hotel companies generally or in Britain in particular, but it illustrates well what is involved and a possible approach.

The personnel officer is one of several specialists reporting directly to the general manager; he is particularly concerned with employment policies, with broad issues of employment in the

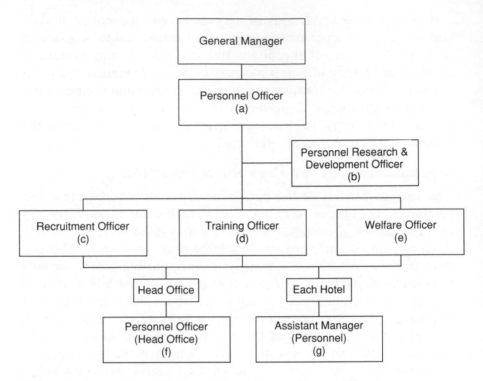

**Figure 8**   Organization of Personnel Function in a Group of Hotels

**Table 17**
Schedule of Personnel Responsibilities in a Group of Hotels

| Position | Responsible to | Responsible for |
|---|---|---|
| (a) Personnel Officer | General Manager | All aspects of the personnel function |
| (b) Personnel Research & Development Officer | Personnel Officer | Job analysis and evaluation, research, records, statistics |
| (c) Recruitment Officer | Personnel Officer | Recruitment and preliminary selection |
| (d) Training Officer | Personnel Officer | All aspects of training |
| (e) Welfare Officer | Personnel Officer | Health, welfare, safety, including employee hostels |
| (f) Personnel Officer (Head Office) | Personnel Officer | All aspects of the personnel function in respect of head office personnel and hotel management |
| (g) Hotel Assistant Manager (Personnel) | Hotel Manager | All aspects of the personnel function in respect of personnel in the hotel |

company, and with the management of his department. The day-to-day operation of the department is divided between several key subordinates within the department and those with personnel responsibilities in individual hotels. One of the key subordinates is responsible for the personnel function of head office employees, hotel managers and assistant managers.

The central personnel department provides a service to the head office and to the hotels in the group. The allocation of responsibilities for personnel matters to an assistant manager in each hotel implies that that person is the group personnel officer's representative in the hotel, but with a direct line of responsibility to the hotel manager.

## Organization of Training

The training division of the personnel department aims to contribute to:

- improving employees' knowledge, skills and attitudes to work;
- increasing output and sales;
- improving recruitment;
- increasing employees' loyalty,
- improving the image of the Company in the outside world;
- reducing breakages, waste of materials and misuse of equipment;
- reducing accidents;
- reducing absenteeism;
- reducing labour turnover;
- reducing stresses on management.

The organization of the training division is shown in outline in Figure 9 and in Table 18.

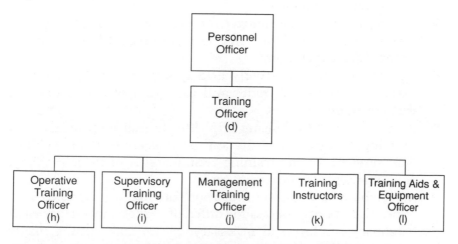

**Figure 9** Organization of Training Function in a Group of Hotels

**Table 18**
Schedule of Training Responsibilities in a Group of Hotels

| Position | Role |
| --- | --- |
| (d)  Training Officer | Directs and coordinates all training and maintains close liaison with Recruitment and Welfare Officers, Personnel Officer (Head Office) and Hotel Assistant Managers (Personnel) |
| (h)  Operative Training Officer | Is responsible for supervision and coordination of all operative training below the level of assistant head of department |
| (i)  Supervisory Training Officer | Is responsible for supervision and coordination of all training above operative and below assistant manager level, i.e. head and assistant head of department training |
| (j)  Management Training Officer | Is responsible for supervision and coordination of all management training above head of department level |
| (k)  Training Instructors | Are specialist trainers in food production, food and drink service, housekeeping, reception and clerical services, providing instruction at all levels under the supervision of and in cooperation with training officers |
| (l)  Training Aids & Equipment Officer | Is responsible for production, maintenance and storage of all aids and equipment, including operational and training manuals |

## Functions of the Training Division

In order to achieve its aims, the training division has the following main functions:

- to formulate a training policy for the approval of the General Manager and the Board and to keep them regularly informed of its implementation;
- to prepare an annual budget for the approval of the General Manager and the Board and to report regularly to them on income and expenditure;
- to identify quantitatively and qualitatively the training requirements for all grades and categories of employees and keep them under review;
- to maintain close liaison with educational institutions and training centres, assess the appropriateness of their facilities and services for the training requirements of the Company, and to arrange for new courses;
- to establish and operate induction, orientation, refresher and other appropriate courses for different grades and categories of Company employees as necessary, and to make arrangements for their attendance;

● to cooperate with appropriate Officers of the personnel department in establishing and maintaining an inventory of management and supervisory personnel and those suitable for developing into such positions, with a view to providing for systematic development of existing and new managers and supervisors;

● to establish and administer training schemes for all grades and categories of employment;

● to maintain adequate premises for purposes of training administration and instruction;

● to prepare operating and training manuals and other publications, teaching aids and other necessary material for employee training;

● to maintain all necessary procedures for training within the Company;

● to represent the Company in all matters concerned with training both within and outside the Company and advise the General Manager and the Board on all such matters.

Throughout the course of our research it has become apparent to us that hoteliers regard human resources to be the single most important issue facing the industry into the next century.

It is recognised that the human resource problems will show a regional variation. In developed countries there will be labour availability problems; in developing countries – and especially those with expanding tourism and hotel industries – there will be problems of education and training for the industry.

The financial resources that need to be devoted to human resources need to be increased and must be viewed as a worthwhile long term investment in the future.

Horwath and Horwath, *Hotels of the Future*

Hotels tend to be labour intensive, because they normally require a high labour contribution in the provision of various facilities and services to their guests. This is reflected in high labour costs, which represent a high proportion of the operating costs of hotels in most regions and countries. Labour productivity is about the relationship between output and the labour resources employed to produce that output. Labour productivity is, therefore, important to hotels. It is a major influence on the competitiveness of an hotel in its markets and on the viability of the business.

## Measures of Labour Productivity

Measures of labour productivity relate output to labour input, and three main types are physical, financial and combined physical/financial measures:

- physical measures relate physical units of output to numbers employed or hours worked;
- financial measures relate output measured in financial terms to payroll;
- physical/financial measures relate output measured in financial terms to numbers employed or hours worked.

Physical meaures are normally specific to particular types of business; financial and combined physical/financial measures can be applied to different types of business, and comparisons can be drawn between them.

Recent annual reports of Horwath International no longer provide all data required to illustrate these measures for the regions and countries shown elsewhere in this book. The illustrations in this chapter use data for the main regions drawing on *Worldwide Hotel Industry* for the late 1980s and data for a number of European countries drawing on *European Hotel Industry* for the early 1990s.

> There have always been two fundamental ways of widening business profit margins. One is by increasing demand for a service or product and the other is by reducing fixed and/or variable costs. Each approach has commonly been regarded as distinct and unrelated to the other . . . However, adopting either market or cost strategies is too limited an approach to hotel productivity . . . it is fundamental to the successful management of productivity in hotels to accept that a reciprocal relationship exists between demand and supply, inputs and outputs, market strategies and cost strategies. Hence there is a need for hotels to be more than simply cost- or market-oriented, but to be both simultaneously.
>
> Stephen Ball *et al.* in *Hospitality Management*, Vol. 5, No. 3

## Physical Measures

Simple physical measures of labour productivity in hotels sometimes relate the room or bed capacity of the hotel and the numbers employed, as shown in Tables 19 and 20 and Figure 10.

| Greece | 0.5 |
| Germany | 0.7 |
| Netherlands | 0.8 |
| Portugal | 0.8 |
| Switzerland | 0.8 |
| France | 0.9 |
| United Kingdom | 0.9 |
| Ireland | 1.0 |

**Figure 10** Employees per Room in European Hotels, 1992

A more meaningful ratio is the number of employees to occupied rooms or to guests, which links employees' output to the volume of business. A similar approach may be adopted on a departmental basis, when the number of rooms serviced by a maid or the number of covers served by a waiter or waitress are calculated.

**Table 19**
Employees per Room in Hotels in Main Regions[a]

|  | 1986 | 1987 | 1988 |
|---|---|---|---|
| Africa and the Middle East | 1.0 | 1.0 | 1.1 |
| Asia and Australasia | 1.0 | 1.2 | 1.5 |
| Europe | 0.7 | 0.7 | 0.7 |
| North America | 0.6 | 0.7 | 0.6 |
| Latin America/Caribbean | 1.2 | 1.1 | 1.3 |

[a] All figures are medians and rounded.
*Source*: Based on *Worldwide Hotel Industry 1987, 1988, 1989.*

**Table 20**
Employees per Room in Hotels in Selected European Countries[a]

|  | 1990 | 1991 | 1992 |
|---|---|---|---|
| Austria | 0.7 | 0.5 | n.a. |
| France | 0.6 | 0.7 | 0.9 |
| Germany | 0.8 | 1.0 | 0.7 |
| Greece | 0.7 | n.a. | 0.5 |
| Ireland | 1.1 | 1.1 | 1.0 |
| Netherlands | 0.5 | 0.7 | 0.8 |
| Portugal | 0.9 | 0.8 | 0.8 |
| Switzerland | 0.9 | 0.9 | 0.8 |
| United Kingdom | 1.1 | 1.0 | 0.9 |

[a] All figures are arithmetic means and rounded.
*Source*: Based on *European Hotel Industry 1991, 1992, 1993.*

These measures give a broad indication of productivity levels and trends for an individual hotel, but have to be interpreted with care in comparisons between hotels, which may differ in the range and type of facilities and services provided.

## Financial Measures: Sales and Payroll

In order to obtain a measure of the relationship between output and labour input which takes into account the value of the output and the cost of the labour input, sales are related to payroll. This relationship may be expressed in one of two ways.

One is calculated as a percentage, which shows payroll as a proportion of sales. Another is an index, calculated by dividing payroll into sales; the index represents the number of times the payroll is covered by sales or, in other words, the number of sales dollars or pounds generated for each dollar or pound of payroll. These measures are illustrated in Tables 21 and 22.

**Table 21**
Sales and Payroll in Hotels in Main Regions[a]

| | Payroll/Sales | | | Sales/Payroll | | |
|---|---|---|---|---|---|---|
| | 1986 (%) | 1987 (%) | 1988 (%) | 1986 | 1987 | 1988 |
| Africa and the Middle East | 28.3 | 27.3 | 28.4 | 3.5 | 3.7 | 3.5 |
| Asia and Australasia | 29.6 | 26.5 | 27.2 | 3.4 | 3.8 | 3.7 |
| Europe | 34.2 | 34.8 | 34.9 | 2.9 | 2.9 | 2.9 |
| North America | 35.3 | 35.6 | 35.5 | 2.8 | 2.8 | 2.8 |
| Latin America/Caribbean | 29.6 | 25.9 | 26.1 | 3.4 | 3.9 | 3.8 |

[a]All figures are arithmetic means.
*Source*: Based on *Worldwide Hotel Industry 1987, 1988, 1989*.


**Table 22**
Sales and Payroll in Hotels in Selected European Countries[a]

| | Payroll/Sales | | | Sales/Payroll | | |
|---|---|---|---|---|---|---|
| | 1990 (%) | 1991 (%) | 1992 (%) | 1990 | 1991 | 1992 |
| Austria | 36.3 | 42.0 | n.a. | 2.8 | 2.4 | n.a. |
| France | 36.6 | 36.8 | 41.4 | 2.7 | 2.7 | 2.4 |
| Germany | 36.0 | 38.2 | 37.9 | 2.8 | 2.6 | 2.6 |
| Greece | 53.4 | n.a. | 38.1 | 1.9 | n.a. | 2.6 |
| Ireland | 27.5 | 28.1 | 30.0 | 3.6 | 3.6 | 3.3 |
| Netherlands | 36.0 | 38.8 | 38.7 | 2.8 | 2.6 | 2.6 |
| Portugal | 36.0 | 34.8 | 38.2 | 2.8 | 2.9 | 2.6 |
| Switzerland | 41.3 | 40.5 | 42.7 | 2.4 | 2.5 | 2.3 |
| United Kingdom | 29.0 | 31.2 | 31.9 | 3.4 | 3.2 | 3.1 |

[a]All figures are arithmetic means.
*Source*: Based on *European Hotel Industry 1991, 1992, 1993*.

They are widely used in practice as a simple and effective approach to monitoring and controlling labour costs of the whole hotel, and also on a departmental basis. However, sales represent gross output, which may be generated by varying combinations of labour and of goods and services bought in, and, therefore, care needs to be exercised in comparisons between hotels.

## Physical/Financial Measures: Sales per Employee

Most measures used in productivity comparisons, which have a common application to establishments and firms, as well as whole industries and economies, relate output in money terms to numbers employed. A simple and widely used approach is to calculate the amount of sales generated per employee, obtained by dividing total sales by the number employed. This is illustrated in Tables 23 and 24.

**Table 23**
Sales per Employee in Hotels in Main Regions[a]

|  | 1986 (US $) | 1987 (US $) | 1988 (US $) |
|---|---|---|---|
| Africa and the Middle East | 25 400 | 28 500 | 26 000 |
| Asia and Australasia | 32 000 | 31 400 | 18 600 |
| Europe | 44 000 | 52 600 | 58 800 |
| North America | 41 500 | 41 400 | 47 000 |
| Latin America/Caribbean | 18 700 | 15 600 | 16 700 |

[a] All figures are medians and rounded.
*Source*: Based on *Worldwide Hotel Industry 1987, 1988, 1989.*

**Table 24**
Sales per Employee in Hotels
in Selected European Countries[a]

|  | 1990 (ECU) | 1991 (ECU) | 1992 (ECU) |
|---|---|---|---|
| Austria | 57 600 | 52 000 | n.a. |
| France | 64 400 | 64 000 | 73 200 |
| Germany | 51 800 | 49 400 | 54 600 |
| Greece | 28 800 | n.a. | 28 800 |
| Ireland | 31 300 | 32 700 | 35 000 |
| Netherlands | 59 300 | 52 200 | 54 900 |
| Portugal | 28 300 | 35 000 | 35 000 |
| Switzerland | 61 300 | 59 000 | 61 800 |
| United Kingdom | 39 700 | 44 100 | 46 800 |

[a] All figures are arithmetic means and rounded.
*Source*: Based on *European Hotel Industry 1991, 1992, 1993.*

Sales per employee is an adequate measure for monitoring labour productivity in an individual hotel. However, as noted earlier, if output is represented by sales, comparisons between hotels may be affected by the extent to which sales may be generated by those employed or by purchases of goods and services from others.

## Productivity Measures: Value Added Approach

Simple measures described and illustrated so far reveal some interesting relationships, but ignore the extent to which output may be generated by varying combinations of those employed and of goods and services bought in. To overcome this, the concept of value added may be used to identify the separate contribution of labour.

Value added by an individual business is defined as the total value of sales less the cost of purchases of materials and services from others. In most businesses this equals sales less expenses other than payroll, or payroll plus profit.

The ratio of value added to payroll then represents the *net* output generated by a dollar or pound of payroll; value added divided by the number of full-time equivalent employees represents the *net* output per employee.

Tables 25 and 26 show the approach for hotels in the main regions and in selected European countries.

**Table 25**
Value Added (VA) Labour Productivity Ratios in Main Regions[a]

|  | Sales (US $) | Exps (US $) | VA (US $) | Payroll (US $) | Profit[b] (US $) | VA ratio |
|---|---|---|---|---|---|---|
| Africa and the Middle East | 1000 | 475 | 525 | 284 | 241 | 1.8 |
| Asia and Australasia | 1000 | 450 | 550 | 272 | 278 | 2.0 |
| Europe | 1000 | 393 | 607 | 349 | 258 | 1.7 |
| North America | 1000 | 418 | 582 | 355 | 227 | 1.6 |
| Latin America/Caribbean | 1000 | 477 | 523 | 261 | 262 | 2.0 |

[a] All figures are arithmetic means.
[b] Gross operating income before fixed charges.
*Source*: Based on *Worldwide Hotel Industry 1989*.

**Table 26**
Value Added (VA) Labour Productivity Ratios in Selected European Countries[a]

|  | Sales (ECU) | Exps. (ECU) | VA (ECU) | Payroll (ECU) | Profit[b] (ECU) | VA ratio |
|---|---|---|---|---|---|---|
| France | 1000 | 335 | 665 | 414 | 251 | 1.6 |
| Germany | 1000 | 363 | 637 | 379 | 258 | 2.5 |
| Greece | 1000 | 419 | 581 | 381 | 200 | 2.9 |
| Ireland | 1000 | 526 | 474 | 300 | 174 | 1.6 |
| Netherlands | 1000 | 339 | 661 | 387 | 274 | 2.4 |
| Portugal | 1000 | 390 | 610 | 382 | 228 | 1.6 |
| Switzerland | 1000 | 360 | 640 | 427 | 213 | 1.5 |
| United Kingdom | 1000 | 399 | 601 | 319 | 282 | 1.9 |

[a] All figures are arithmetic means.
[b] Gross operating income before fixed charges.
*Source*: Based on *European Hotel Industry 1993*.

## Some Ways to Higher Productivity

Productivity measures provide a means to monitoring productivity levels and trends, and to comparing them between hotels and departments, with a view to identifying reasons for differences, and taking steps to improvement.

Although annual ratios for the hotel and for each significant department are a useful starting point, it is clear that for many hotels annual figures conceal wide variations between different parts of the year. It is, therefore, desirable to monitor changes in productivity for periods for which basic input data are readily available, on a quarterly, monthly or weekly basis.

When interpreting the calculated ratios in comparisons, the reasons for differences between hotels and departments and between different periods can be normally identified to the factors that determine hotel staffing, described in Chapter 8. Over short periods of several weeks or months, the incidence of demand may be the only variable. Over a year or so, some changes in productivity may result from changes in most of the factors listed except size, ownership and age and layout of the buildings. Over a longer period all the influencing factors may change and generate changes in productivity.

The traditional view about increasing labour productivity is that it is largely related to the substitution of capital for labour, by machines replacing men. Whatever scope there may be for this in hotels, there are other means to improved productivity in the short and medium term:

- A major scope lies in an examination of the extent to which highly labour-intensive guest services continue to meet an economic demand, and in the elimination of those which do not, or their provision by non-personal methods. In many hotels beds are 'turned down' at night; yet, the bulk of hotel guests do not have beds 'turned down' at home; it is expensive in maids' time; it intrudes into guests' privacy. Tea and coffee making equipment and bar units in rooms tend to be preferred by many guests to floor service.

- As the incidence of demand results in much idle time in hotels, there is often much scope for improving the utilization of employees' time through the definition of jobs, work scheduling, and multi-function staffing, when the same employee performs more than one role or task in a working day.

● Concurrently an improvement in the quality of staff may be achieved through improved recruitment, selection and training, and through financial and other incentives to better performance.

## Productivity Standards

For practical operational purposes, simple productivity standards can be set in terms of payroll levels for different levels of business. The volume of business is normally expressed in terms of occupancy for rooms and in terms of sales for food and beverages and for other departments of the hotel. In practice at least three levels have been found necessary in most situations. The first level denotes the minimum staffing necessary for the hotel to operate; the third level denotes the staffing necessary for a high volume of business; between the two a progression in payroll is allowed as the volume of business increases. The simplified example in Table 27 illustrates the approach for an hotel with high volume sales of more than £100 000 in any period of four weeks.

**Table 27**
An Example of Productivity Standards for an Hotel

| | Rooms | | Food | | Beverages | | Miscellaneous | |
|---|---|---|---|---|---|---|---|---|
| Level | Occupancy | Payroll | Sales | Payroll | Sales | Payroll | Sales | Payroll |
| **1 Low** | 30% or less | £8000 | £15 000 or less | £7000 | £10 000 or less | £4000 | £5000 or less | £3000 |
| **2 Medium** | For each 10%+ | +£1000 | For each £2500+ | +£1000 | For each £2000+ | +£500 | For each £1000+ | +£500 |
| **3 High** | 70% or more | £12 000 | £25 000 or more | £11 000 | £20 000 or more | £6500 | £10 000 or more | £5500 |

How closely an hotel can match payroll to a given level of occupancy or sales depends on the flexibility management has in adjusting the number of employees and hours worked to changes in demand, and this is often limited, particularly over short periods. Employment legislation allows variations in hours worked by employees to a different extent in different countries. Local conditions in the labour market provide varying scope for the employment of casual, part-time and temporary staff, and the scope for this may vary between different departments of the hotel. However, overtime working does enable payroll variations without changes in numbers employed, and relatively few hotels experience frequent, entirely unpredictable fluctuations in the volume of business.

It is clear that the more payroll can be adjusted to the volume of sales, the greater the prospect for improvement in labour productivity. Productivity standards set in these terms have the effect of focusing on the critical relationship between the volume of business and payroll. But standards should be set individually for each hotel, in the light of all its market and operating conditions, rather than applying synthetic formulae to a number of hotels, in which the particular circumstances of the individual hotel may be neglected.

Labour productivity is of major importance for firms and industries and for the whole economy. Through its effect on output, it is a major influence on the viability of economic activities and ultimately on living standards. It is also a major influence on the competitive position of firms and industries in their markets and on the country's international competitiveness.

The employment share of hotel and catering services in the (UK) economy exceeds significantly their share of national output, indicating that they are labour intensive.

The highest turnover per person employed is generated by public houses, the lowest by hotels, restaurants and related activities.

S. Medlik, *Tourism and Productivity*

## Computers in Hotels

In the 1960s and 1970s rapid development of electronic data processing extended the use of computers to many walks of life and some of their most fruitful applications have been in service industries, in accounting, banking and retailing, as well as in hotels. More recently microelectronic technology brought their more widespread use within reach of smaller hotel operations. Microelectronic technology now makes possible cheap, compact and reliable electronic devices with a performance that was previously only possible from bulky and expensive mainframe computers – that is the significance of what has come to be known as the microprocessor revolution.

The new technology is *fast* and speed is important in hotels – in responding to a guest, travel agent or tour operator inquiring about room availability, in effecting a reservation, in linking the reservation with the registration of guests, their charges, and the settlement of accounts.

The new technology is *accurate* and accuracy is important in hotels. The sale of a drink affects cash or a guest's bill, the liquor stock, and the revenue analysis of the hotel – it should affect all three to exactly the same extent.

The new technology is becoming *cheap* to use, cheaper than ordinary office machinery, and with rising costs of clerical labour in hotels, the scope for saving may be considerable.

The new technology, therefore, also has a major contribution to make to hotel productivity. The main applications of computers in hotels are being extended from their established role in reservation systems to front office procedures and guest accounting, to purchasing, stock control and general accounting functions of hotels, as well as other aspects of hotel operations, to form integrated management information systems, which enable the whole business to be closely coordinated and monitored.

Table 28 shows the proportions of hotels contributing to Horwath International reports which used computers in various aspects of their operations in the late 1980s. By location, city centre hotels generally make greater use of computers than resort and other hotels. By region, European hotels tend to employ computers on the whole to a greater extent than hotels in other regions.

**Table 28**
Computer Use in Hotels

| | Reservations (%) | Guest accounting (%) | Point of sales[a] (%) | General accounting (%) | Keys[b] (%) | Energy[c] (%) |
|---|---|---|---|---|---|---|
| All hotels | 72.3 | 66.2 | 51.7 | 72.8 | 17.1 | 22.6 |
| City centre | 77.2 | 74.9 | 64.9 | 79.3 | 21.0 | 24.4 |
| Resort | 72.5 | 68.8 | 50.0 | 77.5 | 18.8 | 18.8 |
| Other | 70.6 | 61.0 | 43.2 | 68.5 | 12.3 | 26.7 |
| Africa and the Middle East | 37.5 | 45.0 | 40.0 | 65.0 | 10.0 | 15.0 |
| Asia and Australasia | 64.4 | 66.7 | 68.9 | 71.1 | 11.1 | 20.0 |
| Europe | 88.0 | 86.7 | 64.0 | 88.7 | 27.3 | 25.3 |
| North America | 79.1 | 69.8 | 57.1 | 72.2 | 18.1 | 30.7 |
| Latin America/Caribbean | 56.4 | 45.6 | 33.3 | 66.7 | 5.3 | 7.0 |

[a] Point of sales terminals for food and beverage outlets.
[b] Electronic card keys.
[c] Computerized energy management.
*Source*: Based on *Worldwide Hotel Industry 1989*.

A major development of recent years has been a rapid growth of computer reservation systems (CRS), also called automated reservation systems, especially in the United States, and central reservations systems. Developed initially by airlines, the interactive electronic data systems provide direct access through terminals not only to airline but also hotel and other operators' computers, to establish product availability, make reservations and print tickets or confirmations. Of major current and future significance are developing links between computers of hotel chains and major airline systems.

# PART IV

Hotel Support Services

Several aspects of hotel products, markets and marketing are considered in this book, before and after the reader reaches this chapter devoted to marketing. They provide both an introduction and a follow-up to the discussion of marketing in this chapter. It is, therefore, appropriate to set this chapter in the context of the various references to aspects of marketing earlier and later in this book, with a view to linking the various parts.

Chapter 1 relates hotel and travel development, places hotels in the total accommodation market, and examines influences on hotel location. In Chapter 2 hotel facilities and services are described as hotel products, their users as hotel markets, and the marketing concept is introduced. In Chapter 3 hotel products and markets enter into the policies, philosophies and strategies of the business. The main hotel products are considered in some detail in Chapters 4-6, and aspects of marketing are referred to in the context of hotel organization and staffing in Chapters 7–9.

The products and markets of small hotels, hotel groups and of international hotel operations, and how each of them approaches marketing, receive attention in Chapters 13–15. Chapter 13 contrasts the products, markets and the marketing of small and large hotels, and identifies the particular marketing strengths and weaknesses of the small hotel. Chapter 14 highlights marketing economies among the most important advantages of large-scale hotel operations, and marketing as providing a particular scope for centralization in hotel groups. Chapter 15 suggests that this is also the case where the groups operate internationally, and includes illustrations of the relative importance of particular products and markets for hotels in selected regions and countries.

There are several books concerned with various aspects of hotel marketing and some of those published in Britain are listed as suggested further reading to this chapter. In view of this and the breadth of the subject, this chapter aims to provide a general outline of the role and scope of the marketing function in hotels rather than to deal with its techniques, and the reader is referred to those texts mainly concerned with marketing for greater detail.

> . . . markets vary. Americans may ask you to dine with them at 6 p.m. (or earlier), Britons at 8 p.m., and I have been invited to dinner in Spain at 10 p.m. History, religion and tradition cause marketing differences. Most sensible people like to sit down and relax over a drink. We 'crazy' Britons prefer to stand up when we drink our pints in a pub. On the Continent of Europe good service is a leisurely meal, in America slow service is often considered bad service. Some countries start a meal with coffee, others never have coffee till the end of the meal . . .
>
> Melvyn Greene *Marketing Hotels and Restaurants into the 90s*

## From Production to Sales to Marketing

Several phases may be distinguished in the evolution of consumer markets including markets for hotel services.

The *first phase* is characterized by a shortage of available goods and services when demand is in excess of supply. There is no sales problem; what is produced can also be sold; the main problem is to increase output. This gives rise to a seller's market and a production orientation on the part of the seller, and has been apparent in many hotel markets at particular times: for example, during the industrialization of most countries, and as recently as the late 1970s and the 1980s in London, Paris, and other capital cities.

The provision of new capacity, technical progress and increased productivity lead to the *second phase*, in which higher real incomes also generate increasing purchasing power. This has occurred first with goods and then with various services. A greater supply then exceeds demand and leads to a buyer's market and a sales orientation on the part of the seller. It is to this phase that may be traced the introduction of sales offices in hotels, as falling occupancies and empty banqueting rooms call for a sales effort.

In the *third phase* a further growth in capacity and output is normally accompanied by a further growth in incomes leading to what has become known in the developed world as the affluent society. It leads to a realization of the need for goods and services to be produced to match consumers' needs, giving rise to a buyer's market and a marketing orientation. Increasingly consumers' needs become the starting point in the planning, design and provision of goods and services, in hotels and elsewhere, because selling alone may not be enough in itself to secure profitability.

Not all hotel markets necessarily undergo these three phases consecutively or in step with each other. But the basic pattern has been from a seller's market and production orientation, through a buyer's market and sales orientation, to a buyer's market and marketing orientation. The key characteristics of the three phases have been the growth in output and capacity on the one hand and the growth of the market on the other hand, accompanied by typical responses on the part of the producers.

## The Marketing Concept

The British Chartered Institute of Marketing has defined marketing as follows:

> Marketing is the management function which organizes and directs all those business activities involved in assessing and converting customer purchasing power into effective demand for a specific product or service and in moving the product or service to the final customer or user so as to achieve the profit target or other objectives set by the company.

In this definition the marketing function is seen not merely as a department of the business, but as coordinating all aspects of the business, and the role of marketing not merely in terms of satisfying demand and generating sales, but including the assessment of consumer demand as a starting point; marketing exists to achieve the overall objectives of the business.

In order to understand marketing in its totality, it is helpful to distinguish between the concept and the various tools and techniques. Conceptually, marketing is a philosophy in the conduct of a business. It is based on a belief that sustainable profitability can only be achieved by identifying, anticipating and satisfying customer needs and desires.

Marketing is not synonymous with selling. Selling focuses on the needs of the seller, marketing on the needs of the buyer. Selling is preoccupied with the seller's need to convert his product into cash, marketing with the idea of satisfying the needs of the customer by means of the product.

In this chapter selling is seen as one of several elements of total marketing activity, which is described later on in terms of the marketing cycle.

> The paradox is that when the marketing concept is observed and carried through in the entire planning process of a new service, the sales effort required in the long run should be minimal. Where great emphasis on sales is required, it usually means that the marketing concept has been disregarded; it is an enormous task to try and sell something which people neither need nor desire. This does not mean that marketing replaces sales, but that they are complementary to each other. If marketing establishes what people need, then the sales function demonstrates that their needs can be fulfilled.
>
> Roger Doswell, *Towards an Integrated Approach to Hotel Planning*

## Special Features of Hotel Marketing

Marketing is first and foremost about matching products and markets and in this sense the marketing of hotel services is in principle no different from the marketing of other consumer products. But there are special features of hotel products and markets and hence of hotel marketing.

For most users hotel rooms are a means to an end and not an end in itself and the demand for them is what is known as derived demand – the reason for their use may be a business visit or a holiday or something else but rarely the room itself, and the same applies to some extent to other hotel services.

The availability of the most important hotel product, the hotel room, is fixed in time and place. In the short term the number of rooms or beds on offer cannot be significantly changed and location is part of the highly perishable product, which cannot be stored for future sale or follow the customer. The demand for hotel accommodation and other services fluctuates from day to day, from week to week, and from one part of the year to another. A waste occurs when demand falls and there is a definite upper limit to the volume of business in a period of peak demand.

Hotel investment is primarily an investment in land and buildings and interior assets. The bulk of the capital invested in the fixed assets of the hotel, combined with the continuity of hotel activity, gives rise to high fixed costs, which have to be covered irrespective of the volume of business. Three key factors are, therefore, critical to a successful hotel operation – the right location, correct capacity, and a high level of utilization. All of them imply marketing decisions – first in the conception of the hotel and in its operation subsequently.

In the conception of the hotel, marketing can contribute first through a market feasibility study to assess the demand. A study may identify the best market opportunity for an hotel, a gap in the market, a location or choice between alternative locations, for a particular hotel concept; or, given a particular location, a study can determine the most appropriate hotel concept. The translation of the concept into an operational facility then takes place through product formulation and development. In the operation of the hotel, marketing can contribute through a continuous process of market research, product development, promotion, selling, monitoring and review – the stages of a marketing cycle, which is described later in this chapter.

In the planning of a new hotel, there is full scope for the adherence to the marketing concept from the outset. In an existing hotel, there is often an important distinction between the short- and long-term marketing tasks. In the short term the marketing task may be to adjust customers' wants to available facilities and services, but the long-term task is to modify the facilities and services to the customers' wants.

In the short run our existing facilities and services are given within narrow limits. We may research the market to see which market segments are or could be attracted to them, make such adjustments to our products as are possible, but the main effort is likely to focus on promotion and selling. With low occupancies and low utilization of restaurants, bars and function rooms, in the short run the sales effort becomes dominant. But it is no excuse for doing just that; it is both necessary and possible to proceed with changing the products: to establish who our customers could be and what their needs are (market research), and to formulate and develop products meeting their needs (product formulation and development). This approach ultimately calls for less sales effort, which is then designed to demonstrate to people that their needs can be met; it is of particular importance in hotels.

Marketed commodities and articles are concrete, physical and capable of measurement; most of them can be inspected and many of them even tried out before purchase. Services are less tangible and hotel services particularly so. Hotel services cannot be easily defined and described in terms of clearly measurable products and their qualities. They are often bought individually or as part of a package, and they may be bought directly by the user or through an intermediary, for example, a travel agent. In hotels, as in other walks of life, it is necessary to make it easy to buy – only more so.

## The Marketing Cycle

Hotel marketing as defined earlier in this chapter begins with an assessment of the existing and potential markets for hotel products. This activity known as *market research* is concerned with providing management with information about markets and products in such a way as to contribute to systematic decision-making. We have seen earlier that the contribution may be both to the development of new hotel facilites and services and to improving existing ones, by identifying the customers and their needs in relation to the particular products offered or to be offered by the hotel.

The next element of the marketing cycle is *product formulation and development*. With adequate information about the market it is possible to identify accurately the particular segments of the market served or to be served by the hotel. The formulation and development of the products to match the identified market segments includes both the range and type of hotel facilities and services and pricing. Where this takes place consciously and systematically, it is possible to achieve a high degree of match between products and markets, because particular products have been shaped for particular defined markets. Where products are developed without market research, the market often tends to shape itself to the product.

Most new products are brought to the attention of the buyer and existing ones are kept in his awareness through *promotion*. In this a broad distinction may be drawn between three sets of methods. Advertising covers the use of the press, radio and television, films, posters and other paid-space or -time media. Public relations include all those efforts other than advertising, such as editorial publicity, intended to create and maintain a favourable image of the hotel and its products. Merchandising is point-of-sale promotion of particular significance in hotel restaurants and bars through packaging, display and presentation. The above activities are supported by brochures, signs and other promotional material and activities. Their combination gives the promotional mix of the hotel, which draws on sales records and which provides a stimulus to sales.

However, marketing achieves the objectives of the hotel only when the room has been booked for the guest, a table reserved in the restaurant, and the function arrangements have been agreed with the organizer. Accomplishing sales places *selling* in the marketing cycle. It may be performed by sales staff whose sole concern is direct selling, but in most successful hotels the receptionists, waiters and other staff in direct contact with the customer are also salesmen.

*Monitoring of performance and review* constitutes the final element of the marketing cycle. It is concerned with comparisons of actual results with plans and budgets and with evaluating the effectiveness of the marketing effort, with a view to providing an informed basis for changes and adjustments in market and product policies and strategies of the hotel.

What has been outlined here as the marketing cycle corresponds closely to the marketing mix, which is commonly described in marketing literature in terms of four variables – product, price, promotion, place (the four Ps).

## Marketing Resources

It is of interest to see what resources are devoted by hotels to marketing. An indication is provided for hotels contributing to Horwath reports in the early 1990s in Tables 29 and 30.

**Table 29**
Marketing Expenses as a Ratio of Hotel Sales
in Selected Regions and Countries[a]

|  | 1990 (%) | 1991 (%) | 1992 (%) |
|---|---|---|---|
| **Africa and the Middle East** | | | |
| Africa | 2.4 | 2.3 | 2.7 |
| Middle East | 3.6 | 2.9 | 3.1 |
| **Asia and Australia** | | | |
| Asia | 4.0 | 4.6 | 5.1 |
| North Asia | 3.2 | 3.6 | 3.7 |
| Australia | 5.4 | 5.9 | 6.4 |
| **Europe** | | | |
| Continental Europe | 3.2 | 3.5 | 3.8 |
| United Kingdom | 3.2 | 3.4 | 3.1 |
| **North America** | | | |
| Canada | 5.3 | 5.7 | 8.1 |
| United States | 6.4 | 7.3 | 7.5 |
| **Latin America/Caribbean** | | | |
| Mexico | 10.1 | 8.2 | 7.6 |
| South America | 4.5 | 3.6 | 4.0 |
| Caribbean | b | b | 5.7 |

[a] All figures are medians.
[b] Included in South America.
*Source*: Based on *Worldwide Hotel Industry 1991, 1992, 1993.*

**Table 30**
Marketing Expenses as a Ratio of Hotel Sales
in Selected European Countries[a]

| | Payroll and related expenses | | | Other expenses | | |
|---|---|---|---|---|---|---|
| | 1990 (%) | 1991 (%) | 1992 (%) | 1990 (%) | 1991 (%) | 1992 (%) |
| Austria | 0.8 | 1.2 | n.a. | 2.7 | 3.1 | n.a. |
| France | 1.2 | 1.4 | 1.6 | 2.9 | 2.5 | 3.1 |
| Germany | 0.8 | 0.9 | 1.0 | 2.8 | 2.8 | 3.0 |
| Greece | 0.5 | n.a. | 0.8 | 1.3 | n.a. | 2.5 |
| Ireland | 0.8 | 0.8 | 1.1 | 2.0 | 2.4 | 2.7 |
| Netherlands | 0.8 | 1.9 | 1.6 | 2.8 | 2.2 | 2.6 |
| Portugal | 1.0 | 1.1 | 1.6 | 2.1 | 2.4 | 3.2 |
| Switzerland | 1.2 | 1.2 | 1.2 | 3.1 | 2.9 | 2.9 |
| United Kingdom | 0.9 | 0.8 | 0.8 | 3.1 | 2.7 | 2.6 |

[a] All figures are medians.
*Source*: Based on *European Hotel Industry 1991, 1992, 1993.*

The particular definition of marketing adopted is based on the *Uniform System of Accounts for Hotels*, which explains what is covered as follows:

> The efforts of a hotel to obtain and to retain customers for its products and services includes many activities. Among them are: building the image of the hotel, developing an awareness by the customer of the hotel's products, and stimulating customers to patronize its various service outlets. These activities are interrelated and make up what is generally termed the marketing effort of a company. In the schedule . . . the various expenses associated with the marketing program are listed. Combined, they show the result of using all of the techniques of merchandising, selling, promoting and public relations by both the internal staff and various outside agencies, to produce business for the hotel.

Marketing includes payroll and other expenses of the relevant activities. Until recently, costs of a reservation system and travel agency commissions were charged to the rooms department. However, current Horwath reports follow the eighth revised edition of the *Uniform System*, which recognizes that these costs are elements of the overall marketing activity of the hotel, and are more appropriately charged to marketing.

As shown in Table 29, in the early 1990s most hotels contributing to Horwath International reports spent on average between 2 and 8 per cent of their total revenue on marketing activities as defined earlier; for European hotels the range was narrower, as shown in

Table 30. Manpower resources devoted to marketing shown in Table 31 indicate ratios of more than two to more than four employees per 100 rooms in most regions and countries, with a particular focus on sales.

**Table 31**
Marketing Employees in Hotels
in Selected Regions and Countries[a]

| | Sales | | | Other | | |
|---|---|---|---|---|---|---|
| | 1990 | 1991 | 1992 | 1990 | 1991 | 1992 |
| **Africa and the Middle East** | | | | | | |
| Africa | 3.0 | 3.0 | 2.9 | 0.9 | n.a. | 0.8 |
| Middle East | 2.3 | 1.8 | 2.4 | 0.3 | n.a. | n.a. |
| **Asia and Australia** | | | | | | |
| Asia | 2.8 | 3.0 | 2.9 | 1.5 | 1.2 | 0.9 |
| North Asia | 2.1 | 2.0 | 2.1 | 1.0 | 0.9 | 0.8 |
| Australia | 1.7 | 1.5 | 1.8 | 0.5 | 0.9 | 0.7 |
| **Europe** | | | | | | |
| Continental Europe | 1.6 | 1.8 | 1.6 | 1.0 | 1.1 | 0.9 |
| United Kingdom | 2.0 | 1.9 | 1.9 | 0.9 | 0.9 | 0.8 |
| **North America** | | | | | | |
| Canada | 2.0 | 1.9 | 2.0 | n.a. | 0.2 | n.a. |
| United States | 2.1 | 2.3 | 1.6 | 0.7 | 0.9 | 0.7 |
| **Latin America/Caribbean** | | | | | | |
| Mexico | 3.0 | 2.4 | 2.3 | 1.3 | 1.3 | 0.6 |
| South America | 2.0 | 2.5 | 2.2 | 1.1 | 2.2 | 1.0 |
| Caribbean | b | b | 1.9 | b | b | 0.8 |

[a] All figures are medians of numbers of full-time equivalent employees per 100 rooms.
[b] Included in South America.
*Source*: Based on *Worldwide Hotel Industry 1991, 1992, 1993*.

However, these figures may underestimate total marketing costs which, some would argue, include not only reservation costs and commissions paid to intermediaries, but also the cost of discounts to tour operators and others, in order to achieve a particular volume of business.

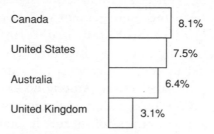

Canada    8.1%
United States    7.5%
Australia    6.4%
United Kingdom    3.1%

**Figure 11**   Marketing Expenses in Hotels, 1992

## Yield and Quality Management

In recent years hotels in common with other types of business have been increasingly adopting yield management – the concept and techniques concerned with the maximization of profit and revenue. Two particular statistics illustrated in Table 32 are yield and discount rates of hotels in selected regions and countries.

**Table 32**
Yield and Discount Rates in Hotels

|  | *Yield*[a] (%) | *Discount* (%) |
|---|---|---|
| **Africa and the Middle East** | 40.1 | 19.5 |
| **Asia and Australasia** | 40.4 | 23.7 |
| **Europe** | | |
| France | 48.2 | 40.5 |
| Germany (FR) | 38.8 | 42.6 |
| Portugal | 31.5 | 44.0 |
| Switzerland | 87.7 | 25.8 |
| United Kingdom | 41.3 | 39.8 |
| **North America** | | |
| Canada | 44.2 | 32.1 |
| United States | 55.2 | 16.8 |
| **Latin America/Caribbean** | 28.3 | 22.6 |
| City centre | 43.0 | 35.6 |
| Resort | 32.2 | 42.1 |
| Other | 40.6 | 19.6 |

[a] $\dfrac{\text{Rooms sold}}{\text{Rooms available for sale}} \times \dfrac{\text{Average rate of rooms sold}}{\text{Average rate protential}}$

*Source*: Based on *Worldwide Hotel Industry 1989*.

The yield percentage shows the proportion of potential revenue hotels are realizing. The discount percentage is the difference between the potential rack rate and the average rate actually paid by guests.

Another growing concern of marketing significance on the part of hoteliers has been the management of quality. The systematic process consists of several stages: determining the guests' requirements; designing hotel facilities and services to meet them; operating the hotel in conformity with the established standards; monitoring the guest satisfaction. Among hotel companies Holiday Inns has pioneered the recognition of the importance of quality in ensuring guest satisfaction and of its role in marketing. A national series of guidelines to companies on what is required of a quality system is provided by the British Standards Institution in BS 5750. (ISO 9000 is the international equivalent of BS 5750.)

> You all know the old 'rule' about a new hotel. First year it loses money. The second year it breaks even, then the third year shows a reasonable profit. The same applies to a lot of marketing effort and cost. If only a one year viewpoint is taken on marketing results, this seriously inhibits recovery from the present problems, and restricts long-term profit growth. My case is that basically both operating and marketing management must have a marketing strategy looking ahead two to three years.
>
> Melvyn Greene, *Marketing Hotels and Restaurants into the 90s*

## Hotels in the Total Tourist Product

More often than not hotel accommodation and other hotel products are parts of a total tourist product, which covers, from the point of view of the tourist, the whole experience from the time he leaves home to the time he returns. Airline seats and hotel beds may be seen as individual products by their suppliers but, as far as the tourist is concerned, they are only product components; for the tourist what he buys is a composite product, an amalgam of attractions, transportation, accommodation, entertainment and other activities.

The amalgam or package the tourist buys is seen most clearly in the case of inclusive tours, where the tour operator or another organizer brings together all the elements of a holiday, which he promotes and offers for sale as a single product at one inclusive price. However, all tourists buy packages, whether they use travel agents or not, and whether they buy the various components separately or as an inclusive tour, and this applies to holidays as well as to business trips.

This has important implications for hotel marketing, for increasingly hotel beds – and other hotel facilities and services – cannot be successfully marketed in isolation. They are supplied by many separate individual operators, each of whom provides only a part of what the tourist buys and often in relatively small quantities. We have seen earlier that for most hotel users hotel rooms are a means to an end and not an end in itself; they also normally need other means to an end, and their concern as consumers is the end rather than the means.

In these circumstances it becomes increasingly important to realize that all suppliers, including hoteliers, are in the main serving to facilitate what is seen by the consumer as part of one overall tourist experience. It follows that the interests of all suppliers of facilities, including hoteliers, are more effectively served, if they recognize their respective roles in and contributions to the total product, and if they organize their respective marketing efforts accordingly. This is not to say that they need to submerge their identities and integrate under one control. But it does mean that a great deal of promotion of independent individual hotels, transport and related companies may be less effective than coordinated efforts of those concerned with the promotion of the total tourist products.

Three types of coordination are required for effective marketing in travel and tourism, where components of the total product are provided by separate producers:

●    at the destination it is the role of the official tourist organization to formulate and develop tourist products based on the destination and to promote them in appropriate markets;
●    at the generating end it is the role of the tour operator to assemble component services into packages and to promote them and sell them as single products;
●    it is the role of individual operators to formulate, develop and supply their products as parts of a total tourist product.

Just as it is necessary to question whether airlines are really in the business of selling seats in the air (a transport experience), it is necessary to question whether hotels are really in the business of selling rooms (an accommodation experience).

# *Property Ownership and Management*

The general organization and administration, staffing and productivity of the facilities and services described in Part II of this book, are discussed in Part III. Part IV is devoted to hotel support services; it begins with the discussion of marketing in Chapter 10 and concludes with a discussion of finance and accounts in Chapter 12. All this activity takes place in buildings and the business of hotels is, therefore, concerned, in addition to markets, money and people, also with the ownership and management of property.

## Property Ownership

An investment in hotels is first and foremost an investment in land and buildings, which represent the dominant assets of hotels. Other fixed assets are:

● plant and equipment, including such major items as air conditioning, boilers, lifts, and heavy kitchen equipment;
● furniture, furnishings, and small equipment;
● china, glass, linen and cutlery.

Accordingly there is a dual nature of investment in hotels – as an investment in land and buildings and an investment in interior assets. This distinction has been recognized in three principal ways in recent years.

First, the building shell may be owned by a developer, sometimes as part of some larger project, and leased to an hotel operator on a rental basis. This is also implied by some hotel groups, which apply internal rentals to hotels owned by them; in this way the hotel profits are assessed after taking into account the notional rental of the land and building.

Secondly, hotel companies make use of sale-and-lease-back arrangements as a means of financing the investment, which reduces the capital requirement for the hotel operator.

Thirdly, interior assets may be also leased by the hotel operator rather than bought, thereby also reducing the capital requirement.

There are, therefore, various arrangements as to who is involved in property ownership and in hotel management. An hotel operator may invest in the property represented by land and buildings or enter into a leasing arrangement and invest only in the interior assets, or an operator may enter into a management contract without any direct capital investment.

## Property Operation and Maintenance

In large hotels and in hotel groups normally a senior person is ultimately responsible for technical services who may be variously described as the technical services, buildings and services, or works director, officer, or superintendent, or simply as chief engineer, or by some such title. In large organizations the technical services may be subdivided between those responsible for buildings, for engineering, and for other services.

Technical considerations involved in property operation and maintenance and in the related subject of energy are outside the scope of this book. Although they may be the direct concern of hotel management in smaller hotels, they are specialist activities normally entrusted to specialist staff and sometimes 'contracted out'. Moreover, they are well documented in many texts, and several of those published in Britain are listed as suggested further reading.

Property operation, maintenance and energy costs are costs of hotel operation, as distinct from the capital investment outlay on the assets. They are, therefore, appropriately included in hotel profit and loss statements. What role these costs play in different parts of the world is illustrated in tables based on hotels contributing to Horwath International reports in the early 1990s.

In the *Uniform System of Accounts for Hotels* property operation and maintenance includes costs of repairs and maintenance of buildings, plant and equipment, furniture and furnishings, as well as the maintenance of grounds, related wages and salaries, and work let out on contract. The costs incurred by hotels contributing to Horwath International reports in the early 1990s are shown as a ratio of total sales in Tables 33 and 34.

**Table 33**
Property Operation and Maintenance Costs as a Ratio of Hotel Sales
in Selected Regions and Countries[a]

|  | 1990 (%) | 1991 (%) | 1992 (%) |
|---|---|---|---|
| **Africa and the Middle East** | | | |
| Africa | 6.6 | 5.8 | 6.5 |
| Middle East | 5.6 | 5.1 | 5.6 |
| **Asia and Australia** | | | |
| Asia | 4.3 | 5.0 | 4.2 |
| North Asia | 3.9 | 3.9 | 3.9 |
| Australia | 4.8 | 4.3 | 5.0 |
| **Europe** | | | |
| Continental Europe | 3.6 | 4.0 | 4.8 |
| United Kingdom | 3.1 | 3.3 | 3.2 |
| **North America** | | | |
| Canada | 5.6 | 5.8 | 5.5 |
| United States | 5.5 | 5.4 | 5.7 |
| **Latin America/Caribbean** | | | |
| Mexico | 8.9 | 8.8 | 9.4 |
| South America | 7.0 | 6.1 | 6.3 |
| Caribbean | b | b | 7.6 |

[a] All figures are medians.
[b] Included in South America.
*Source*: Based on *Worldwide Hotel Industry 1991, 1992, 1993*.


**Table 34**
Property Operation and Maintenance Costs as a Ratio of Hotel Sales
in Selected European Countries[a]

|  | Payroll and related expenses | | | Other expenses | | |
|---|---|---|---|---|---|---|
|  | 1990 (%) | 1991 (%) | 1992 (%) | 1990 (%) | 1991 (%) | 1992 (%) |
| Austria | 1.5 | 2.0 | n.a. | 2.0 | 2.0 | n.a. |
| France | 1.4 | 1.8 | 2.7 | 2.4 | 6.1 | 3.1 |
| Germany | 2.1 | 2.2 | 2.1 | 3.1 | 4.7 | 3.0 |
| Greece | 5.4 | n.a. | 2.6 | 2.3 | n.a. | 2.2 |
| Ireland | 1.1 | 1.1 | 1.3 | 2.5 | 3.2 | 4.4 |
| Netherlands | 1.5 | 2.3 | 2.0 | 3.1 | 3.4 | 3.4 |
| Portugal | 2.6 | 2.5 | 3.1 | 2.4 | 4.5 | 2.6 |
| Switzerland | 1.9 | 1.8 | 2.0 | 2.7 | 3.4 | 2.4 |
| United Kingdom | 1.2 | 1.2 | 1.2 | 2.8 | 5.0 | 2.6 |

[a] All figures are medians.
*Source*: Based on *European Hotel Industry 1991, 1992, 1993*.

The main factors, which influence these costs, are the age and size of the hotel – older hotels tend to spend more of their revenue on property operation and maintenance than newer ones, and so do relatively smaller hotels in comparison with large ones. When interpreting the above figures, it should be borne in mind that the hotels on which the figures are based are typically large modern hotels.

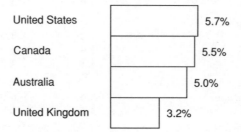

| United States | 5.7% |
| Canada | 5.5% |
| Australia | 5.0% |
| United Kingdom | 3.2% |

**Figure 12**   Property Operation and Maintenance Costs in Hotels, 1992

Staffing ratios in property operation and maintenance activities in different regions and countries are shown in Table 35, which highlights major differences between hotels in Australia, and Europe and North America, and those in other regions.

**Table 35**
Property Operation and Maintenance Employees in Hotels
in Selected Regions and Countries[a]

|  | *1990* | *1991* | *1992* |
|---|---|---|---|
| **Africa and the Middle East** | | | |
| Africa | 16.1 | 15.1 | 11.0 |
| Middle East | 9.1 | 7.5 | 10.0 |
| **Asia and Australia** | | | |
| Asia | 8.3 | 7.6 | 7.2 |
| North Asia | 7.1 | 6.5 | 5.7 |
| Australia | 3.4 | 2.1 | 2.2 |
| **Europe** | | | |
| Continental Europe | 3.0 | 2.9 | 3.0 |
| United Kingdom | 3.9 | 2.6 | 3.5 |
| **North America** | | | |
| Canada | 2.0 | 2.4 | 1.8 |
| United States | 2.5 | 3.0 | 2.4 |
| **Latin America/Caribbean** | | | |
| Mexico | 12.1 | 12.5 | 12.0 |
| South America | 10.3 | 6.3 | 4.2 |
| Caribbean | b | b | 11.7 |

[a] All figures are medians of numbers of full-time equivalent employees per 100 available rooms.
[b] Included in South America.
*Source*: Based on *Worldwide Hotel Industry 1991, 1992, 1993.*

# Energy

In the *Uniform System of Accounts for Hotels* energy costs include the cost of electrical power, fuel, steam and water. These costs are shown for hotels contributing to Horwath International reports in the early 1990s as a ratio of total revenue in Tables 36 and 37. Overall energy costs account for a higher proportion of hotel revenue in climates where air conditioning is an essential requirement in first class hotels, than in cold climates where heating represents the major part of energy consumption.

**Table 36**
Energy Costs as a Ratio of Hotel Sales in Selected Regions and Countries[a]

|  | 1990 (%) | 1991 (%) | 1992 (%) |
|---|---|---|---|
| **Africa and the Middle East** | | | |
| Africa | 5.7 | 5.1 | 7.0 |
| Middle East | 3.7 | 3.1 | 3.3 |
| **Asia and Australia** | | | |
| Asia | 6.3 | 5.7 | 4.7 |
| North Asia | 4.4 | 4.8 | 4.6 |
| Australia | 3.5 | 4.0 | 3.9 |
| **Europe** | | | |
| Continental Europe | 3.4 | 4.0 | 3.9 |
| United Kingdom | 3.3 | 4.3 | 4.3 |
| **North America** | | | |
| Canada | 3.4 | 3.7 | 5.1 |
| United States | 4.7 | 4.6 | 6.0 |
| **Latin America/Caribbean** | | | |
| Mexico | 5.7 | 5.9 | 5.7 |
| South America | 5.1 | 6.0 | 6.5 |
| Caribbean | b | b | 11.3 |

[a] All figures are medians.
[b] Included in South America.
*Source*: Based on *Worldwide Hotel Industry 1991, 1992, 1993*.

Energy costs represent a significant element of hotel costs and their control has been receiving particular attention in most regions and countries in recent years. This is reflected in the latest edition of the *Uniform System*, which indicates the kind of statistical information to be produced by monitoring demand and consumption in physical units as follows:

| Water | cubic feet or gallons | Purchased steam | pounds |
| Electricity | kWH | Natural gas | 100 cubic feet |
| Electrical demand | kW | L.P. gas | pounds |
| Oil | gallons | Heating degree days | |
| Coal | tons | Cooling degree days | |

**Table 37**
Energy Costs as a Ratio of Hotel Sales in Selected European Countries[a]

| | 1990 (%) | 1991 (%) | 1992 (%) |
| --- | --- | --- | --- |
| Austria | 3.2 | 3.8 | n.a. |
| France | 2.9 | 2.4 | 2.7 |
| Germany | 4.0 | 4.5 | 4.4 |
| Greece | 6.4 | n.a. | 4.2 |
| Ireland | 3.5 | 3.6 | 4.1 |
| Netherlands | 2.3 | 2.5 | 2.6 |
| Portugal | 5.0 | 4.9 | 5.1 |
| Switzerland | 2.7 | 3.0 | 3.0 |
| United Kingdom | 3.3 | 4.3 | 4.3 |

[a] All figures are medians.
*Source*: Based on *European Hotel Industry 1991, 1992, 1993.*

**Figure 13**   Energy Costs in Hotels, 1992

## Hotels and the Environment

Over the past two or three decades concern has arisen over the effects of human activities on the environment. The key problems have been identified as global warming, ozone depletion and acid rain, as well as the depletion and pollution of land and water natural resources.

Hotels are increasingly recognizing the need for using energy and other resources responsibly and controlling consumption, as a social responsibility as well as good business. Eleven leading international companies are now members of the International Hotels Environment Initiative, which has developed practical guidelines for hotels, based on a manual produced by Inter-Continental Hotels. The International Hotel Association seeks to assist hoteliers in reconciling environmental issues with competitive pressures. Hotels figure prominently in the work of the World Travel and Tourism Environment Research Centre at Oxford Brookes University, which monitors, assesses and communicates effective environmental strategies in travel and tourism.

The financial position and performance of an hotel are reflected in two key statements – the balance sheet and the profit and loss account. The balance sheet gives a view of the position of the business at a particular point in time, for example, at the end of a year, about the ways money has been raised and about the forms it takes in the business. The profit and loss account shows the revenue and the costs and expenses incurred in earning that revenue, for a given period, a week, a month, or a year.

Several main groups of people are interested in the information these two statements convey – in particular the owners, lenders and managers – and it is possible to distinguish between two outlooks – long-term and short-term.

*Owners and long-term lenders* are interested in the sustained profitability of the hotel. They look for evidence of this at the return on investment, as an indication of the use the business makes of its assets, and at the relationship between owners' capital and loans, as an indication of the way in which risks are spread, as well as at the long-term trends.

*Short-term lenders and trade creditors* take a more limited view and wish to be particularly satisfied that the hotel can meet its current obligations. They look for evidence of this at its current assets, particularly cash and those readily convertible into cash, and at the extent of its current liabilities, which have to be met in the short term.

*Management* has responsibilities to investors and to both long-term and short-term creditors. Therefore, management has to consider all the aspects which are of interest to these parties, but management is concerned also with planning and day-to-day control of the business. The financial statements it needs have to be more detailed and more frequent than those required by others, to enable it to direct the hotel and to monitor its progress.

Both financial statements are of interest to all these different parties. However, normally the balance sheet is of particular value to owners and lenders, whilst the profit and loss account is of greater value to management. In this chapter illustrations of hotel financial statements provide a basis for the description of their main features and of the financial characteristics of the hotel business.

## The Hotel Balance Sheet

There is no universal agreement on the presentation of the balance sheet and one variation arises in its horizontal form: for example, in Britain assets are shown on the right-hand side and capital and liabilities on the left-hand side; in some countries the balance sheet is part of the double entry system of accounts and the reverse applies. The simplified example in Table 38 is a vertical statement of an hotel with an investment of £1 000 000, with the assets listed first, and how they are financed next.

**Table 38**
Balance Sheet as at 31 December 19-

| | | | |
|---|---|---|---|
| Fixed assets | | | |
| Land and buildings | £675 000 | | |
| Plant and equipment | £100 000 | | |
| Furniture and furnishings | £ 75 000 | | |
| China, glass, cutlery, linen | £ 30 000 | £880 000 | |
| | | | |
| Current assets | | | |
| Stocks | £ 30 000 | | |
| Debtors and repayments | £ 60 000 | | |
| Cash | £ 30 000 | £120 000 | £1 000 000 |
| Owner's capital | | £600 000 | |
| Long-term loans | | £300 000 | |
| Current liabilities | | | |
| Creditors and accruals | £ 30 000 | | |
| Bank overdraft | £ 70 000 | £100 000 | £1 000 000 |

*Note:* The form of ownership and taxation have been ignored in this illustration.

## Balance Sheet Ratios and Analysis

The different forms of capital employed in the business are represented by the various types of assets used in the hotel, and balance sheet items are grouped into sections – fixed and current assets, equity, and long- and short-term liabilities.

*Hotel investment requirements* are basically of three types. Short-term capital is required for up to a year for operating and minor capital expenditure; medium-term finance is required for several years for internal fixed assets; long-term finance, for more than a few years, is required for land and buildings.

The grouping of assets into fixed and current reflects the *investment intensity*, which is normally very high in hotels, because the bulk of hotel investment is in land and buildings and other fixed assets. The investment intensity – the relationship between fixed and current assets – has important implications; for example, it contributes to high fixed costs of hotel operation through depreciation and other expenses of property ownership. Current assets comprise cash and other items convertible into cash in the normal course of business, such as stocks, which tend to be small in the hotel business, because they are converted into debtors or cash relatively quickly. It is, therefore, not uncommon to find 80-90 per cent of the total investment in hotels in the form of fixed assets, giving an investment intensity of 4 or more.

The distinction between *long- and short-term liabilities* emphasizes their different nature and the time scale of the obligations. The former is a form of total financing of the hotel; the latter are in the main amounts owed to suppliers and, unless they include such short-term borrowing as bank overdrafts, they tend to be relatively small in hotels.

The difference between the total assets and the total liabilities is the *equity or the net worth of the business*. It represents the owners' capital, and according to the form of ownership, is represented by the shareholders' capital in a company or by capital accounts for partnerships and individual proprietorships. Initially money can be put in the business by the owners or contributed by others. Subsequently capital can be increased by the owners putting in more or by profits not drawn out by owners; more can be also borrowed as loans.

The relationship between equity and liabilities is known as *capital gearing*. The ratio is calculated by dividing the net worth by total liabilities or, where current liabilities fluctuate, the net worth is divided by the long-term debt only, and indicates the strength of the capitalization. Both investors and lenders are interested in the return on total assets irrespective of the source of funds, but capital gearing influences their respective risks. Where the proportion of indebtedness is high in relation to owners' capital, small changes in profit may have a significant impact on the return available to owners, as interest on loans and instalments have to be paid in any case when due. The extent of desirable gearing in hotels, as in other types of business, depends to a greater extent on whether the rate of return earned by the hotel exceeds the rate of interest paid on the loan.

Another important relationship exists between current assets and current liabilities, because the latter have to be paid in the main out of the former. The excess of current assets over current liabilities represents the net working capital of the business. The *current ratio*, as it is called, is calculated by dividing current liabilities into current assets, and represents a measure of the liquidity of the business. Where stocks are high, it is preferable to exclude them and to calculate the current ratio on the basis of other current assets. But in hotels a simple ratio of 1.00 is normally considered acceptable in view of the commonly low stocks in relation to total current assets and their rapid turnover.

## The Hotel Profit and Loss Statement

A condensed statement showing the main revenue and expense headings is normally used for financial reporting purposes to satisfy legal requirements, but a more detailed structured statement is helpful for management and operational control purposes. A form of this statement, known as the summary operating statement, without the inclusion of intermediate profit levels, is shown in Table 39, where the figures give the performance of an hotel with a total revenue of £2 000 000.

The main *profit and loss concepts* are:

- revenues are classified by product/department, showing the revenue mix;
- costs and expenses are classified by type of cost and expense into cost of sales, payroll, other direct expenses, undistributed operating expenses, and fixed charges;
- cost of departmental sales (opening stock + purchases – closing stock) is related to each category of sales (food, beverages, minor operated departments);
- departmental payroll is related to each category of sales (rooms, food and beverages, minor operated departments);
- direct departmental expenses incurred in the operation of a department are allocated to that department;
- operating expenses relating to the whole hotel, which are not distributed to departments, are distinguished from fixed charges related to assets and capital.

**Table 39**
Profit and Loss Summary Operating Statement
for the Year to 31 December 19-

|  | £000 | £000 |
|---|---|---|
| Revenue | | |
| Rooms | 968 | |
| Food | 560 | |
| Beverages | 256 | |
| Minor operated departments | 148 | |
| Rentals and other income | 68 | 2 000 |
| Departmental cost of sales | | |
| Food | 188 | |
| Beverages | 61 | |
| Minor operated departments | 73 | 322 |
| Departmental payroll and related expenses | | |
| Rooms | 166 | |
| Food and beverages | 297 | |
| Minor operated departments | 38 | 501 |
| Other departmental expenses | | |
| Rooms | 98 | |
| Food and beverages | 95 | |
| Minor operated departments | 30 | 223 |
| Undistributed operating expenses | | |
| Administration and general | 188 | |
| Marketing | 68 | |
| Property operation, maintenance, energy | 200 | 456 |
| Fixed charges | | |
| Rent | 120 | |
| Depreciation | 80 | |
| Other fixed charges | 136 | 336 |
| Net profit | | 162 |
| (before income taxes and gain or loss on sale of property) | | |

The summary operating statement enables profit margins to be established at various levels, after certain expenses but before others, and the net profit. There are several *profit levels*:

- *departmental gross profit* for food, beverages, and minor operated departments (revenue less cost of sales);
- *departmental net margin* for rooms, food and beverages, and minor operated departments (revenue less prime cost, i.e. cost of sales and payroll);
- *departmental operating profit* for rooms, food and beverages, and minor operated departments (revenue less direct expenses, i.e. prime cost and other departmental expenses);

- *hotel operating income* (the sum of departmental profits plus rentals and other income);
- *hotel operating profit* (operating income less undistributed operating expenses);
- *hotel net profit* (operating profit less fixed charges).

## Profit and Loss Ratios and Analysis

The relationship between revenues and costs and expenses of operated departments, which account for the first three profit levels above, were presented for rooms, food and beverages, and minor operated departments in Tables 5, 9 and 12 in Chapters 4, 5 and 6. The next three profit levels relate to the hotel as a whole. All six profit levels based on Table 39 are summarized in Table 40.

**Table 40**
Profit and Loss Summary Operating Statement
for the Year to 31 December 19-
Showing Profit Levels

| | Rooms (£000) | Food (£000) | Beverages (£000) | MOD[a] (£000) | Total (£000) |
|---|---|---|---|---|---|
| Revenue | 968 | 560 | 256 | 148 | 1932[b] |
| *Less* Departmental cost of sales | – | 188 | 61 | 73 | 322 |
| DEPARTMENTAL GROSS PROFIT | 968 | 372 | 195 | 75 | 1610 |
| *Less* Departmental payroll and related expenses | 166 | 297 | | 38 | 501 |
| DEPARTMENTAL NET MARGIN | 802 | 270 | | 37 | 1109 |
| *Less* Other departmental expenses | 98 | 95 | | 30 | 223 |
| DEPARTMENTAL OPERATING PROFIT | 704 | 175 | | 7 | 886 |
| *Add* Rentals and other income | | | | | 68 |
| HOTEL OPERATING INCOME | | | | | 954 |
| *Less* Undistributed operating expenses | | | | | 456 |
| HOTEL OPERATING PROFIT | | | | | 498 |
| *Less* Fixed charges | | | | | 336 |
| HOTEL NET PROFIT | | | | | 162 |
| (before income taxes and gain or loss on sale of property) | | | | | |

[a] Minor operated departments.
[b] Excluding Rentals and Other Income (£68 000), before this is added to Departmental Operating Profit.

A number of ratios may be calculated from the information in Table 40:

- for each operated department each element of cost (cost of sales, payroll, other departmental expenses) may be expressed as a percentage of departmental sales;
- for each operated department each profit margin (departmental gross profit, net margin, operating profit) may be expressed as a percentage of departmental sales;
- for the whole hotel rentals and other income, undistributed operating expenses, and fixed charges may be expressed as a percentage of total hotel revenue;
- for the whole hotel operating income, operating profit, and net profit may be expressed as a percentage of total hotel revenue.

**Table 41**
Ratios of Costs, Expenses and Profit Margins
to Departmental Sales and to Hotel Revenue

| | Rooms (%) | Food (%) | Beverages (%) | Minor operated Depts (%) | Total[a] (%) |
|---|---|---|---|---|---|
| Revenue | 100 | 100 | 100 | 100 | 100 |
| *Less* Departmental cost of sales | – | 34 | 24 | 50 | - |
| DEPARTMENTAL GROSS PROFIT | 100 | 66 | 76 | 50 | - |
| *Less* Departmental payroll and related expenses | 17 | | 36 | 26 | - |
| DEPARTMENTAL NET MARGIN | 83 | | 33 | 25 | - |
| *Less* Other departmental expenses | 10 | | 12 | 20 | - |
| DEPARTMENTAL OPERATING PROFIT | 73 | | 21 | 4 | 44.3 |
| *Add* Rentals and other income | | | | | 3.4 |
| HOTEL OPERATING INCOME | | | | | 47.7 |
| *Less* Undistributed operating expenses | | | | | 22.8 |
| HOTEL OPERATING PROFIT | | | | | 24.9 |
| *Less* Fixed charges | | | | | 16.8 |
| HOTEL NET PROFIT | | | | | 8.1 |

[a] Including rentals and other income.

In Table 41 the information in Table 40 is expressed in the form of ratios. Departmental costs and expenses and profit margins are related to corresponding departmental sales. Costs and expenses and profit margins of the whole hotel are related to total hotel revenue.

*Particular ratios are of significance for particular purposes.* They enable each element of cost and expense to be controlled for each operated department in relation to the sales of that department. Similarly, total departmental costs and expenses, as well as undistributed operating expenses and fixed charges can be controlled in relation to total hotel revenue. They can also assist in decision-making. For example, the prime cost of the food and beverage operation covers both the cost of food and beverages and the labour cost, including preparation and service, and is an important concept in menu pricing. Thus in any comparison between fresh foods and convenience foods, the prime cost and the departmental net margin ratios provide a basis for evaluating alternative means of operation.

When the departmentalization of the operating statement follows the responsibilities of the hotel organization structure, it is possible to equate the various profit levels with individual responsibilities. In this only items of revenue and expenditure which can be controlled by individuals are attributed to them. Thus for example:

- *departmental gross profit* is the responsibility of the chef, head barman, telephone supervisor;
- *departmental operating profit* is the responsibility of the front hall manager and the food and beverage manager;
- *hotel operating profit* is the responsibility of the hotel manager.

Hotel control is facilitated not only by the structure of the financial statements and the amount of detail and analysis they contain, but also by the frequency with which they are produced. This varies as between different hotels, but it is common to find that the following are produced together with related ratios and with supporting schedules:

- daily statement of revenue;
- weekly statement of cost of sales and payroll;
- monthly operating statement of revenue, costs and expenses;
- quarterly balance sheet.

## Hotel Operating Profit

The most significant profit level for management purposes is the hotel operating profit, i.e. the level after all operating costs and expenses have been deducted from hotel revenue, and before fixed charges. This is normally the level for which the responsibility lies with the hotel operational management. The ratios of hotel operating profit achieved by hotels contributing to Horwath International reports in the early 1990s are shown in Tables 42 and 43.

**Table 42**
Hotel Operating Profit as a Ratio of Hotel Sales
in Selected Regions and Countries[a]

|  | 1990 (%) | 1991 (%) | 1992 (%) |
|---|---|---|---|
| **Africa and the Middle East** |  |  |  |
| Africa | 24.0 | 32.7 | 11.4 |
| Middle East | 29.8 | 30.1 | 37.5 |
| **Asia and Australia** |  |  |  |
| Asia | 28.5 | 28.0 | 32.5 |
| North Asia | 21.9 | 14.7 | 18.9 |
| Australia | 4.3 | 1.8 | 7.5 |
| **Europe** |  |  |  |
| Continental Europe | 21.0 | 16.7 | 12.5 |
| United Kingdom | 28.5 | 20.2 | 21.8 |
| **North America** |  |  |  |
| Canada | 11.8 | (1.0) | (4.1) |
| United States | 3.9 | 3.9 | 7.1 |
| **Latin America/Caribbean** |  |  |  |
| Mexico | 6.9 | 12.2 | 3.5 |
| South America | 1.4 | 6.7 | 12.6 |
| Caribbean | b | b | 3.4 |

[a] All figures are medians.
[b] Included in South America.
*Source*: Based on *Worldwide Hotel Industry 1991, 1992, 1993*.

**Table 43**
Hotel Operating Profit as a Ratio of Hotel Sales
in Selected European Countries[a]

|  | 1990 (%) | 1991 (%) | 1992 (%) |
|---|---|---|---|
| Austria | 29.3 | 19.6 | n.a. |
| France | 30.6 | 30.0 | 25.1 |
| Germany | 26.3 | 24.4 | 25.8 |
| Greece | 11.0 | n.a. | 20.0 |
| Ireland | 18.9 | 18.4 | 17.4 |
| Netherlands | 30.0 | 29.5 | 27.4 |
| Portugal | 27.7 | 31.0 | 22.8 |
| Switzerland | 19.5 | 23.4 | 21.3 |
| United Kingdom | 32.4 | 29.4 | 28.2 |

[a] All figures are arithmetic means.
*Source*: Based on *European Hotel Industry 1991, 1992, 1993*.

The achieved operating profit in different regions and countries ranges widely and in some of them fluctuates widely from year to year. Economic recession appears to have affected the performance of hotels in Australia and North America in particular.

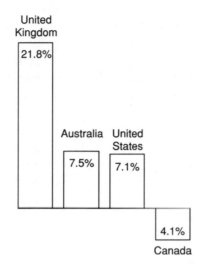

**Figure 14** Hotel Operating Profit, 1992

## Balance Sheet and Profit and Loss Relationships

So far we have considered mainly relationships between two individual items or groups of items within one financial statement. Thus from the balance sheet emerges the investment intensity of the hotel as a relationship between fixed and current assets, the capital gearing as a relationship between owners' capital and liabilities, and the liquidity of the hotel as a relationship between current assets and current liabilities. From the profit and loss statement a multitude of relationships emerges when components of revenue, costs and expenses, and profit margins are related to total or departmental revenue.

However, there are also many points at which *items in the balance sheet and in the profit and loss statement are related* to each other. When assets are used up, they become expenses; for example, fixed assets are depreciated and depreciation becomes an expense; stocks are used up and become the cost of sales. On the other hand revenues create assets; for example, sales generate cash or debtors. Credit purchases create liabilities. Profit increases the net worth of the business and loss reduces it. A meaningful financial analysis of an hotel has to include these relationships between assets, liabilities, income and expenses.

The most important relationship is that between *earnings and assets*, because the ratio of earnings to investment is a measure of the effectiveness of management in employing assets to generate profits. This is a more meaningful measure than return on owners' capital in a total view of the performance of the hotel. Earnings are used in the calculation before deduction of interest, which is not a charge against operations but a charge for the use of a particular form of capital, and in evaluating the use that is made of assets, the source of capital is immaterial.

There are also important relationships between stocks and sales, debtors and sales, and creditors and purchases. The *rate of stock turnover* is calculated by dividing the cost of food, beverages and other sales by the average stock, i.e. the sum of opening and closing stocks divided by two. The rate represents the number of times a particular stock turns over in a year, and is a useful indicator for avoiding over-stocking.

**Table 44**
Liquidity Ratios in Hotels
in Selected Regions and Countries[a]

| | Current ratio | Rate of stock turnover | | Rate of debt turnover[b] |
|---|---|---|---|---|
| | | Food | Beverages | |
| **Africa and the Middle East** | | | | |
| Northern Africa | 1.71 | 15.0 | 2.1 | 11.6 |
| Southern Africa | 1.47 | 14.1 | 3.5 | 8.2 |
| Middle East | 1.81 | 15.6 | 5.7 | 10.8 |
| **Asia and Australasia** | | | | |
| Asia | 1.25 | 24.0 | 3.5 | 10.1 |
| Far East/Pacific Basin | 1.15 | 25.6 | 4.9 | 14.1 |
| Australia | 1.09 | 28.7 | 5.9 | 18.2 |
| **Europe** | | | | |
| Continental Europe | 0.96 | 24.2 | 3.3 | 13.3 |
| Scandinavia | 1.45 | 38.4 | 8.3 | 20.8 |
| United Kingdom | 0.91 | 41.1 | 7.1 | 13.9 |
| **North America** | | | | |
| Canada | 1.92 | 26.3 | 6.9 | 28.6 |
| United States | 1.05 | 24.9 | 5.3 | 15.6 |
| **Latin America/Caribbean** | | | | |
| Latin America | 1.09 | 21.0 | 3.0 | 10.3 |
| Caribbean | 3.38 | 9.2 | 3.5 | 11.0 |

[a] All figures are medians.
[b] Based on total sales.
*Source*: Based on *Worldwide Lodging Industry 1985*.

The speed with which debts are collected from customers is shown by the *rate of debt turnover*, which is measured by dividing credit sales by average debtors, i.e. the sum of opening and closing debtors divided by two; sometimes total sales are used in calculating this ratio rather than credit sales.

Table 44 gives illustrations of several of the ratios, which have a particular bearing on the liquidity of the business for hotels contributing to Horwath International reports in the mid 1980s.

# PART V

Hotel Dimensions

# The Small Hotel

Whether measured by the scale of investment, turnover, number of rooms or beds, numbers employed, or by other criteria, in most countries a large proportion of hotels are small businesses. In this chapter small hotels are described with a view to providing a simple profile of their main distinguishing characteristics.

Hotel ownership offers considerable attractions to people willing to invest money, time and effort in building up a business. It offers economic independence in a business that provides a means of livelihood in an activity full of human interest, and it offers scope for individual flair. As with other small-unit industries, such as agriculture, building, and retail distribution, there are good chances of setting up one's own business in the hotel industry. Since many individuals enter the industry with modest capital and to a great extent use their own financial resources, they tend to do so on a small scale and their hotels remain small.

The nature of the hotel business also helps to explain the importance of the small hotel, because it is concerned with providing personal services. Its size is limited by the size of the market and by the extent of competition. Many markets for hotel services are small and many small markets are served by more than one hotel. Moreover, size is not a requirement of a viable hotel operation, as it is in some other industries.

Most hotels provide more than one product – rooms, meals and refreshments, and sometimes also other services – and they do so in various combinations. It is, therefore, less than satisfactory to define a small hotel for our purposes in terms of a particular room or bed capacity. Such other criteria, as a given level of investment or sales, mean different things in relation to hotels of different standards and price levels, and their values change with time. In this chapter the small hotel is, therefore, seen as an establishment, which is owner-managed through the personal involvement of the proprietor in the day-to-day conduct of the business. This is not the case with all small hotels, but the concept has certain meaningful characteristics as regards ownership and management of the hotel generally, and its financing, organization, staffing and control in particular.

A small hotel defined in this way often has more than minimal capital invested in it, employs non-family labour, and is perceived as a business by its owners. This distinguishes the small hotel discussed here from, for example, a private household providing some holiday accommodation, or a bed and breakfast establishment letting a few bedrooms, without differentiating too sharply between the small hotel and the larger guest house.

## Products and Markets

Independent owner-managed hotels have commonly up to twenty or thirty rooms and less than twice that number of beds, a restaurant or a dining room, and a bar, and sometimes also offer a few other guest facilities and services. Their main distinguishing features are the range and scale of the facilities and services.

Rooms may, but need not necessarily, represent the largest single source of hotel revenue. Some small hotels have relatively extensive restaurant and bar facilities in relation to their room capacity, when they serve local residents and others as well as hotel residents. But in many small hotels these facilities are often used primarily by hotel residents, with restricted meal times and fixed meal charges; hotel residents' bars then usually take the form of lounge bars. Telephone, newspapers and guest laundry are the main and often the only services provided by small hotels, in addition to sleeping accommodation, food and drink. If the hotel caters at all for functions, they are likely to be small meetings, parties, and such family occasions as wedding receptions.

The products of the small hotel relate to its markets, which are likely to be more specialized in a large city with a variety of hotels than in a small town where the hotel may be one of only a few small hotels or the only hotel serving the town. Because of its size, the users of small hotels are individuals and families rather than groups, and few small hotels can accommodate such organized groups as coach tours, which require a minimum room capacity, although some may cater for their meals and refreshments. Like all hotels, if it is open to non-residents, in its catering markets the small hotel is usually in competition not only with other hotels, but also with restaurants, pubs and clubs, and other types of outlet for meals and refreshments.

There is an important difference in the way large and small hotels seek to match their markets and products. Large hotel operators increasingly assess their markets, formulate operations to meet apparent market needs, and set out to sell their hotel products to identified market segments by employing promotion on a large scale. Small hotels tend to approach their markets less formally and more intuitively from their detailed knowledge of their guests' requirements, based on their close contact with them. They tend to adjust their services more readily to the known preferences of their guests and to rely for selling their products more on personal recommendation and repeat visits than on systematic promotion. However, this is a broad generalization: large successful hotels do, of course, pay a great deal of attention to the reactions of their guests and even small hotels can be rarely successful without active promotion.

- Small hotels are not just smaller versions of large hotels. They are fundamentally different and are often 'families' first and business second.

- The survival of small hotels located in disadvantaged areas has more to do with the way the business partners organise their work and non-work activities than the use of marketing skills.

Andy Lowe in *Hospitality Management,* Vol. 7, No. 3

## Ownership and Finance

Traditionally the small hotel has been owned by an individual or a family, and the common legal form of ownership has been an unincorporated firm, a sole trader or sometimes a partnership, but increasingly it is a private company in order to obtain the advantages of limited liability. Although some small hotels are owned by those with other business interests, more often than not the establishment as a place of business, and the firm as a unit of ownership and ultimate control, which raises capital and employs and organizes productive resources, coincide.

We have seen in Chapter 12 that hotels require short-term, medium-term and long-term finance for particular purposes. The dependence of the small hotel on one individual, the owner/manager, and the type of security available for a loan, are among the factors that have tended to mitigate against the availability of external finance from lending institutions. It is common for small hotels to provide most of the finance of all three types from retained profits and from personal savings, sometimes drawn from the realization of other assets, and the main external sources are bank overdrafts and loans; this applies not only to short-term requirements, but also to much fixed capital expenditure. Much longer-term finance is drawn from private sources and from the financial involvement in the business of private individuals who are prepared to lend. Some may become 'sleeping' partners or even directors of private companies, usually confining their participation to their financial stake, and leaving the day-to-day conduct of the business to the owner/manager, who is often the principal owner of the business. Small hotels, therefore, tend to have a high proportion of 'equity' capital, contributed by one or more individuals, and a low proportion of loan capital, contributed by a limited number of sources open to them.

Income to owners of small hotels, unlike those of large ones, accrues in four different ways. In addition to the appreciation of land and buildings and annual profits, the two sources common to both, many owner/managers and their families derive a significant income in kind, because they live on the premises, as well as any salaries they may pay themselves. It is often difficult to differentiate clearly between profit as return on investment and the emoluments of the owners in the form of cash and non-cash benefits, which they derive as a reward for managing the hotel. However, there is much to be said for attempting this at least annually, in order to assess the profitability of the business meaningfully. Using purely financial criteria, the true comparison is what the capital invested in the hotel could earn if invested elsewhere, and what the owners themselves could earn elsewhere for a comparable effort.

## Organization and Staffing

In large hotels ownership and management are normally separate functions, both conceptually and in practice. The business is owned by shareholders. The top management is entrusted by them to directors who in turn delegate the day-to-day conduct of the business to operational management. A managing director may provide a link between the top and operational management, and according to the size of the business there may be several levels of operational management. The operation is divided into departments, in which employees perform more or less distinct tasks, and there may be line managers as well as specialists.

In the small hotel the owner/manager is an entrepreneur who normally combines not only ownership and management but often also the functions of top and operational management in one person. Whatever the legal form of ownership, it is this person who undertakes the investment and the financing of the hotel, decides the objectives and the policies, and is responsible for planning, direction, organization, staffing, and control.

The owner/manager may turn for outside advice and help – and usually does – on accounts and finance, architecture and design, business promotion, law, maintenance of equipment and services, and on other matters, but he or she tends to be to a great extent their own marketer, buyer, personnel officer, as well as the one who organizes and coordinates the hotel facilities and services generally, and who represents the hotel to the outside world.

The scale of operation has two main implications for its organization and staffing: limited departmentalization and the likelihood that it can be supervised without, or with no more than one, intervening level. This may be illustrated with an organization chart of a small hotel with some twenty employees shown in Figure 15.

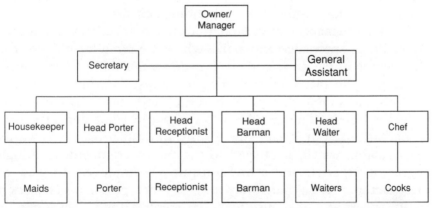

**Figure 15** Organization Chart of a Small Hotel

In this hotel two people assist the owner in the office and the other eighteen have specific but quite wide 'departmental' responsibilities. The office is the nerve centre of the hotel, in which are brought together all the central functions of the hotel, including accounts, purchasing, sales promotion and general administration.

The general assistant has a part in all these directions, as well as in assisting the owner with the overall coordination of the business, but does not have a direct authority over those involved in the six main operational areas. Although each of these has a person in charge, because of their size, these areas represent sections rather than departments in the normal sense of the word.

It is possible to see in this illustration how the division of work may be reduced still further in a small hotel, so that the owner may actually supervise all employees directly. One office may deal with wages, suppliers' invoices, and most other clerical tasks, as well as with the reception of guests, their accounts, and related guest services; food and drink may be served by the same waiters. The majority of employees may be interchangeable: a bookkeeper/receptionist may assist in the bar and the dining room; a porter may attend to guests and their cars and luggage and also serve drinks in the lounge; a waitress may divide her working day between the bar, dining room and the servicing of guest rooms. Such arrangements not only provide flexibility in the deployment of staff and reduce idle time, but may also improve staff job satisfaction through a variety of work. On the other hand, to imitate the large hotel by providing a wide range of services and a departmental structure can destroy the particular advantages the small hotel enjoys, without corresponding benefits.

From the management viewpoint a small hotel operation calls for a breadth of knowledge and skills, which are rarely combined to a high degree in the same person. It reduces the ability of managers to delegate, so that they are engaged almost continuously in the business and so that they perform duties undertaken by employees in larger hotels. The small hotel can avoid rigid departmental demarcations, but it can make only limited progress towards specialization which, if utilized to the full, is conducive to a high degree of expertise and a high output per employee. In view of these factors, a small hotel may provide much personal satisfaction for its owners and often also for those employed in it, but it can be expected to create little innovation in terms of hotel organization and staffing.

## Accounting and Control

Most hotels, however small, keep some accounts, in order to have a record of their transactions with their guests and suppliers, and in order to satisfy certain legal requirements. But for their control small hotels tend to rely on the personal involvement and supervision of the proprietor, rather than on detailed accounting and statistical records. A simplified approach to accounts is adequate and also cost-effective.

Three main basic accounting records satisfy most requirements of most small hotels:

- A *receipts and payments book* records all cash transactions. In the course of business sales accounts and invoices are filed separately and only recorded in the book after payment has been received or made. At the end of the period unrecorded transactions such as outstanding sales accounts, unpaid invoices, prepayments and accruals are taken into account in preparing final accounts.
- A *vistor's tabular ledger* with individual accounts for all resident guests may be extended to include separate accounts for functions, as well as for total cash and credit sales in the restaurant and bar to customers using these facilities without taking up sleeping accommodation. In this way the tabular ledger represents an analysed daily summary of all business done.
- A *wages book*, which includes all employee and related payments, provides a comprehensive record of all payroll transactions.

The proprietors of a small hotel tend to view each hotel product or department as an integral part of the whole and are more concerned with the overall profitability of the hotel than with the relative profitability of its parts. However, different hotel services generate different profit margins, and even a simple breakdown of revenue and expenditure can provide a helpful analysis of performance:

- to indicate the relative profitability of the different parts;
- to establish a basis for monitoring and comparison;
- to enable an assessment to be made of the effect of any changes introduced in operation.

If the basic records are kept in an analysed form, the input data for a meaningful analysis of results are available without much additional effort. It is, therefore, quite easy even for small hotels to produce informative accounts, and to do so more than once a year, from the basic records outlined above. They are helped in this by the relatively small total volume of transactions, many of which are on a cash basis. What is realistic in most small hotels, may be summarized as follows:

- It is is normally adequate to analyse income and certain expenses under no more than four headings: rooms, food, liquor and miscellaneous. The last category is residuary and covers what may be analysed into several separate minor operated departments in a large hotel, but is unlikely to be very significant in a small hotel.
- An extended visitors' ledger can provide analysed details of all revenue.
- Cost of sales data for food and beverages can be derived from an analysed receipts and payments book and adjusted for changes in stock levels, to give the *gross profit*. (Because room sales do not involve the sale of goods, there is no cost of sales for rooms, and miscellaneous sales are not likely to be significant.)
- Each employee is allocated to the department in which he or she is primarily employed, or an employee's payroll cost may be divided between the departments to which he contributes. The balance of profit after the deduction of cost of sales and payroll costs from sales is the *net margin*.

Although in a large hotel the analysis is taken further by deducting from the net margin those other expenses that can be allocated to a department, in order to arrive at the departmental operating profit it is not necessary to proceed beyond the net margin in a small hotel, because this stage tends to account for between a half and two-thirds of the total costs of most hotels and gives a good indication of the profitability of individual hotel facilities and services.

The analysed results produced in this way can then be compared periodically with the budget, with figures for the previous year, or with figures for the previous period, prepared on the same basis, to monitor the performance of the hotel.

For economic reasons apparently hotels became bigger and bigger. Once the developers had paid for the site and the infrastructure it became economic sense to add as many rooms as possible. It did not, however, necessarily make behavioural sense from a guest's point of view and the developers of large hotels lost sight of the human need of being 'loved and wanted'. As we have all heard before, 'in *x* hotel you feel like a number'. This complete ignoring of the needs of guests by developers did, in fact, severely set back the standards of hotelkeeping . . . But what should be the hotel design of the future? Already in the US there is a movement from the massive chain hotels of the sixties and seventies to smaller more personal hotels.

Peter Venison, *Managing Hotels*

# The Future of the Small Hotel

Small business faces particular problems in competition with large firms in most industries and the small hotel business is no exception. Its scope for expansion is limited because it can marshal only limited investment capital from its own cash flow and from external sources. Its resources allow business promotion only on a limited scale and it has to rely for most of its sales on individuals rather than groups. It represents a small buyer in the market and cannot buy in bulk. It may lack management skills, cannot afford to employ specialists, and offers limited career prospects for employees. Its volume of business is too small to secure a high degree of efficiency in its operations, and the limited range of its products makes it vulnerable to external pressures. In other words the small hotel is denied the advantages of size, described in the next chapter in connection with hotel groups.

But the small hotel has few management problems of the large hotel and it often enjoys certain advantages because it is small. The owner/manager can market the hotel with a personal touch and individuality, and to generate a substantial volume of repeat business. He or she is also able to manage the hotel as an individual and to generate a personal loyalty in their employees.

The future of the small hotel, therefore, lies in concentrating on what it can do best and what it alone can do, on the high-quality, individual and personal approach to hotelkeeping, in which the guests and employees find an alternative to the large unit and the large company, and which many of them may prefer. But the small hotel may also need to adapt some of the advantages of the big one to its needs through cooperative action, and by drawing on the assistance which is available to it. Three particular approaches have been prominent in some countries.

One has been the formation of hotel consortia or cooperatives of independent hotels and there are two main types: one is a local group of independent competing hotels in a town or district. When mutual trust and confidence has been established among several hotels, this has led to group marketing, purchasing and other forms of cooperation, securing significant economies for the participants. The other type is a consortium of independent non-competing hotels widely distributed geographically. Their emphasis has been on marketing touring holidays by car and coach and on referral business, but also on common strategies in other directions. To be effective most consortia have set up central offices with full-time staff; these and their activities are financed by members' subscriptions.

The other main development has been the creation of advisory services for small hotels by national hotel associations and by tourist boards. The service organized as a small team of consultants to give practical advice and guidance to small hotel operators performs a similar role for the individual hotel as a management services department does in a large organization for its units or departments.

Small hotels can also benefit, more than large ones, from inter-hotel comparison surveys, which enable them to compare their own performance with other hotels with similar characteristics, and to identify particular operating weaknesses. Evidence from several countries with established surveys indicates that they have been a major stimulus to a critical approach to the examination of hotel operations and to improvements in efficiency.

# *Hotel Groups*

The traditional pattern of an hotel industry made up of individually owned hotels has been changing in many countries for many years and has come to resemble more closely that of other industries, with a small number of companies increasing their share of the market, the remainder being shared by a large number of smaller firms, most of them operating single hotels. The independently owned hotel may be still the dominant firm in the industry, but the growth of the industry has been increasingly associated with hotel groups. The increase in the size of hotel firms has come about by firms building or acquiring hotels in different locations and placing them under central management. The hotels may be grouped within a restricted geographical area or distributed widely within the country or even internationally.

There were more than 30 hotel groups with more than 1000 rooms each in Britain in the early 1990s. The largest, Forte (formerly Trusthouse Forte), accounted for some 30 000 rooms in more than 300 hotels throughout the country, in addition to its interests abroad. Several dozen other groups owned and operated more than one hotel. There were at the time many more groups with more than 1000 rooms in the United States; a number of them exceeded the capacity of Forte in Britain, e.g. Holiday Inn, Marriott and Sheraton, as did Accor hotels in France and the Sol Group in Spain. Leading hotel groups in Britain are shown in Appendix E and leading international hotel groups in Appendix F.

The hotel groups normally operate hotels owned by them or leased by them from their owners to whom they pay a rental. Sometimes they manage hotels as agents for the owners under management contracts, which provide for the payment of expenses, management fees and/or the sharing of profits. The groups may also operate under franchise agreements, which allow one party (the franchisee) to sell a product designed, supplied and controlled by the other party (the franchisor), in return for a fee or a share of profits; in this arrangement an hotel group may be in the role of a franchisor or in the role of a multiple franchisee.

The main purpose of this chapter is to describe the advantages and the problems of hotel groups, the main issues facing them, and their approach to group operation. Hotel group operations under management contracts and under franchise agreements have much in common with any group operation, but both are based on particular agreements between the parties and introduce elements specific to the relationship between them, which are quite distinctive. This chapter is primarily concerned with hotel group operations of hotels owned or leased by the group. Readers with a particular interest in management contracts and franchises are referred to texts on these business relationships listed in the suggested further reading for this chapter.

- Accor is the largest hotel group based in Europe.
- Hospitality Franchise Systems is the largest hotel group based in the Americas.
- New World/Ramada International is the largest hotel group based in Asia.
- Protea Hospitality Corporation is the largest hotel group based in Africa.
- Southern Pacific Hotels is the largest hotel group based in Australia.

(Appendix F)

## Advantages of Groups

The nature of the hotel business and the limits of many hotel markets provide the main explanations for the growth of hotel companies through groups. The advantages, which may accrue to hotel groups are the resulting advantages of size, known as the economies of scale. Some of these, e.g. the technical economies, may apply also to individual hotels, if they are large enough, but their full realization is open particularly to groups of hotels. Groups extend the size to which an hotel firm may grow, economies of scale tend to accompany groups for a long time before pronounced managerial disadvantages set in, and some of the economies, such as those of risk-spreading, are open only to groups. Because economies of scale are available to groups rather than to single hotels, generally a higher profitability is attainable by a group than could be generated by the sum total of its hotels operated independently. The advantages of hotel groups may be summarized as follows.

One of the main *financial economies* is the ability of the group to marshal capital resources from its own cash flow and from external sources. A group may be able to borrow from lending institutions and to do so on favourable terms because it is big and because its hotels provide a good security to its lenders. This is of particular value in financing growth by adding further hotels to the group, in modernizing hotels, and in covering the initial period of operation of new hotels before they become profitable. A group can also deploy its financial resources to advantage by balancing the working capital requirements of its hotels over a period of time and thereby alleviating the strain on individual units caused by seasonality and other fluctuations in revenue and in expenditure.

Because of its size a group can enjoy *marketing economies*. It can create a group image in the market, which may extend to a common name, facilities and standards throughout the group, and it can engage in promoting its hotels together. Individual hotels may to a greater or lesser extent specialize and provide facilities and services complementary to the other hotels, such as conferences. Public relations, advertising and sales promotion can be undertaken with an impact for the whole group. Each hotel within the group can promote other hotels and generate business by onward reservations.

An hotel group has open to it *economies of buying* because it can buy in bulk and negotiate advantageous prices and terms with its suppliers of a wide range of goods and services on behalf of the whole group. A large group can also benefit from central testing of products and from experimenting with different products in its hotels before their use is extended to the whole group.

Management costs need not keep pace with an increase in the volume of business and an hotel group can enjoy *managerial economies*. It can attract high-quality staff through the prospects it can offer within the group and the availability of training schemes, and benefit from an interchange of staff between its hotels. It can also provide centralized services to its hotels and in these it can employ specialists with the time and skills to exploit the advantages of group operation in such areas as finance, personnel, purchasing and marketing.

Various *technical economies* may arise with size in individual large hotels but also in groups, particularly when the hotels are concentrated geographically within a limited area. The volume of business may then make it possible to concentrate such operating facilities as central food production, maintenance and laundry, when reductions in unit costs may be achieved as compared with providing the facilities in individual hotels or buying the services from outside firms.

Last but not least, there may be *economies of risk-spreading*, which enable groups to reduce risk by product and geographical diversification. Hotels that cater primarily for business and for holiday markets tend to have different seasons; some may specialize in functions and others in conferences. A decline in demand for a particular hotel may be offset by a high volume of business in another hotel, and thus even out the fluctuations for the group as a whole, as we have seen above when considering the financial advantages of groups.

It can be seen that the advantages of scale that may accrue to hotel groups arise from several sources: from the weight the group has in markets (whether it is in its markets with customers or suppliers, or in the markets for productive resources, in particular capital and labour); from providing certain services to its hotels; and from operating them as a group. These sources of economies are complementary. But before considering how they may be exploited and what issues they raise, it is necessary to consider the problems hotel groups may experience.

## Problems of Groups

The hotel group shares several main problems with any large organization, especially problems of communications, control and costs.

In order to operate as a group, the centre has to communicate policies, procedures and other matters to individual hotels, which in turn have to communicate information, requests and other matters to the centre. In a closely integrated group individual hotels also have to keep in contact with each other. Unless smooth lines of communication are established and maintained, this can mitigate against the effectiveness of group operation and the attainment of the advantages. Action may be delayed and result in a loss of revenue or additional costs, in time and effort wasted in clearing up misunderstandings, and in antagonism that may be generated.

Whatever the degree of central direction and monitoring of individual units, there is a need for some control to be exercised over the conduct of the hotels, to ensure group decisions being carried out and the accountability of individual hotels for their performance. Unless a clear and effective control mechanism exists, hotels may act against the interests of the group and affect its performance as a whole. However, a complex control mechanism may generate disproportionate costs and affect the initiative and performance of the hotels as well as of the whole group.

A group operation gives rise to its own costs, through the need for communication and control, and through the provision of central services to hotels. If the advantages of group operation are to be realized, it is clear that these additional costs have to be outweighed by the benefits which they bring about, if the group is to produce higher profitability than the individual hotels would if operated independently.

In addition to the quality of the group management, the extent of the above problems depends on three main factors: the number of the hotels in the group, the geographical dispersal of the hotels, and the extent to which the various aspects of the group operation are centralized. The less of each, the less likelihood of these problems being serious. But the smaller the group and the less centralization, the less is also the prospect of the advantages of group operation being realized. The problems arising from the number of hotels and their dispersal may be to some extent overcome by a district or regional structure, but this in itself generates costs. The problems due to centralization can be overcome only by a careful evaluation of the advantages and drawbacks of alternative approaches, by management of high quality, or – by decentralization.

A malaise often found in groups is a hostility on the side of the managers and staff in the hotels towards the group management personnel at the centre. It manifests itself in various ways, but its primary cause is two-fold; first, a feeling that the people at the centre are too remote from the units to understand the problems, and, secondly, the natural resentment of people who consider themselves skilled practitioners of their profession, at being directed from above.

Fenton *et al.*, *Hotel Accounts and their Audit*

... there is often (or often said to be) a failure by a large group to react to local conditions. For example, it is not uncommon for all or most hotels in a group to have a common image, and for the hotels to be sited only in places where that image fits. But if in a particular town conditions change (e.g. traffic patterns, population mix/growth), it is often difficult for the hotel to make a corresponding change in its own patterns or style, because to do so would depart from the group image.

Fenton *et al.*, *Hotel Accounts and their Audit*

The side effects of communication problems are notorious. Paper work tends to increase and diversify, not because it is necessary, but as a self-protective device for people who want it to be seen and provable that they have communicated. Communication also takes time, and often larger groups react more slowly to events than do single unit enterprises.

Fenton *et al.*, *Hotel Accounts and their Audit*

## Scope for Centralization

A group management may adopt a mainly passive ownership role. At its extreme this means the appointment of local managers who are expected to achieve results by their own initiative, with a minimum of central direction, support and supervision. In these circumstances the performance of the group is made up of the more or less independent actions of individual hotels, with a loose monitoring by the owners directly or through a group manager, a managing director, or even a company secretary, with little or no staff of their own. Outside specialists, such as professional stocktakers, may be employed, and the company auditors may perform two roles – that of accountants preparing the accounts of the group and that of auditors verifying the view of the business presented by the accounts; their work may include, in greater or lesser depth, an operational audit.

However, in order to obtain the advantages of group operation, a more positive group management approach is necessary. The group management has to formulate the objectives, policy and operational guidelines, evolve strategies and plan on behalf of the group; it has to direct and coordinate the separate units, and it has to control them financially and in other ways.

The economies of scale do not accrue to the group automatically. Common ownership may bring about certain financial advantages, but to realize most or all the advantages, decisions have to be taken on which functions of the group to centralize and on the extent of centralization of each. The major issue for an hotel group is, therefore, how much to centralize, and the principal functions which offer scope for centralization are:

- accounting and finance;
- personnel services;
- purchasing;
- sales and marketing;
- technical services.

As we have seen, these are the areas in which the main economies of scale lie, and the main influencing factors are the number of hotels and their geographical distribution. Different degrees of centralization are possible in each function: even when centralization is affected, each function has to be divided between the centre and the hotels; how much each does and the relationship between the two are of crucial importance.

However decentralized the group approach may be to *accounting and control*, such aspects as the preparation of the final accounts for the group (even if only as a consolidation of the accounts of individual hotels), capital accounts, cash management and detailed analysis of the financial performance of each hotel, are normally central functions. Beyond these more obvious areas, the main possibilities for centralization arise, depending on circumstances, in accounting for purchases (particularly where purchasing is centralized), payroll (for some or all employees), and credit sales accounts (particularly with such large hotel users as business firms, tour operators and travel agents), stocktaking and internal audit.

At a modest level a centralized *personnel function* is concerned with staffing levels, salary and wage structure, and with employee records. It normally deals with recruitment, selection and placement, sometimes for all employees, sometimes only with particular grades and categories and others are recruited and engaged locally. When the personnel function is more extensive and highly developed, it may cover all conditions of employment, training and welfare, and also employee consultation, negotiation and industrial relations generally.

As substantial economies may be achieved by centralized *purchasing*, few group hotels buy all or most of their supplies directly from any supplier they choose. The centralized purchasing function may be concerned with a varying range of supplies and essentially take one of three basic forms or a combination of the three. In some instances, when the hotels are located in a limited area, supplies are bought for central stores, from which they are distributed to hotels. In the absence of central stores, orders may be placed centrally against requisitions by hotels and delivered directly to hotels. The third form is the placing of orders by individual hotels against centrally negotiated contracts, with nominated suppliers who deliver directly to the hotels.

A wide scope for a group approach exists in *sales and marketing*, where all or some of publicity, advertising and direct sales promotion may be centralized, to project the desired image of the group and to generate sales particularly from large hotel users. When the group is large enough, it can undertake its own market research or commission it from a specialized agency, package its own products and operate a centralized reservation service. Individual local promotion and a centralized approach are normally combined by most groups as being complementary directions aimed at somewhat distinct markets.

There are several *other operations*, which may be carried out by individual hotels, or obtained from specialist suppliers, or provided to hotels in a group as a central facility, if their volume is large enough and if the hotels are close enough to be served centrally. These were earlier referred to as offering scope for technical economies and can be located in one hotel serving others or separately, e.g. various technical services.

## A Concentrated Hotel Group: an Illustration

The aspects discussed in this chapter are illustrated first with an example of an hotel group which operates 18 London hotels with a total of 3500 rooms, 26 restaurants, 28 bars and almost 100 function rooms in these hotels, and which has some 3500 employees. The largest hotels have several hundred rooms and employ several hundred people, the smallest hotels have less than 100 rooms and less than 100 employees. The simplified organization chart of the company is shown in Figure 16.

In this example the central functions of the group below board level and above the level of an individual hotel comprise 165 employees; more than 100 of them are accounted for by a large Estates Department, which employs directly a wide range of maintenance staff.

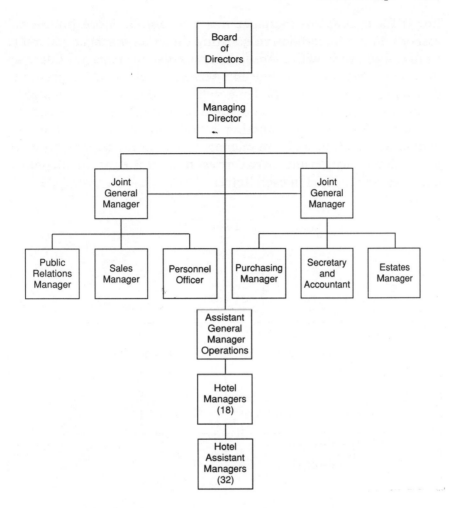

**Figure 16** Organization Chart of a Concentrated Hotel Group

Each general manager is concerned with certain central functions as well as with individual hotel operations through an assistant general manager. Each hotel has a manager and, according to size, between one and three assistant managers. All central functions are linked with the responsibilities of particular managers and assistant managers in the hotels.

The arrangements vary as between individual hotels. Normally the manager retains personal responsibility for public relations and for estate functions, in liaison with the corresponding central departments, and in all but the largest hotels also for one or more other functions, in addition to the general management of the hotel. Each assistant manager has also one or more functional responsibilities in addition to assisting the hotel manager generally: in the large hotels with more than one assistant manager, one may be responsible for sales, one for personnel and one for accounts and purchasing; in the smaller hotels with one assistant manager, all the specialist functions are divided between the manager and the assistant. The personnel function is normally the main or the only responsibility of an assistant manager. This arrangement provides for a direct relationship between each central department and a designated individual in each hotel.

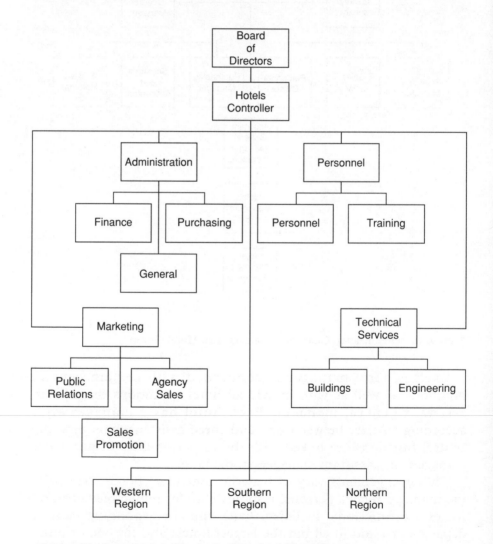

**Figure 17**   Organization Chart of a Dispersed Hotel Group

# A Dispersed Hotel Group: an Illustration

Figure 17 represents an outline organization chart of a group of more than 30 hotels distributed widely over most of England and Wales, with a head office in the Midlands. The hotels range in size from about 50 to about 120 rooms, all of them have a restaurant and a bar, several have more than one restaurant and more than one bar, and all hotels cater for small functions. The group employs some 2000 people.

There are two distinctive features of this organization structure: central departments are grouped into four, bringing together related functions, and the hotels are grouped into three regions, with 10–12 hotels in each region. The hotels controller who reports to the Board of Directors thus has seven senior executives who report to him directly, four in respect of specialist central departments and three in respect of hotel operations.

Because of the wide geographical dispersal of the units, the central departments provide broad policy guidelines and such support services to individual hotel managers as they may require. The regional controllers are concerned with the enforcement of agreed targets and standards and with their monitoring. But within these limits individual managers are allowed relatively wide discretion in the operation of their hotels.

With the growth of international travel and of hotel industries in the less developed countries of the world, there has been a significant growth in international hotel operations. In the broad sense the term describes hotel groups, which operate in more than one country, but it is possible to distinguish between two main types. One is represented by national companies with a head office in a particular country, which engage in hotel operations in that country and in other countries. The other type is multinational companies established by airlines and other interests, which operate hotels in different countries, and in whose case the location of the head office may not be of particular significance. The British owned Forte PLC with its head office in London exemplifies the first type, SAS International Hotels owned by Scandinavian Airlines with its head office in Brussels the second type.

For the first type, which may be described as a national company, international operations offer scope for expansion outside their initial sphere of operations, often on more favourable terms than in their own countries, and for further exploitation of economies of scale, particularly in finance, marketing and risk-spreading through geographical diversification.

Multinational companies seek similar advantages. When airlines participate in international hotel operations they bring together the two main components of the travel product – transportation and accommodation, thereby diversifying their products, as well as often seeking to safeguard their main business, the transportation of passengers, by providing accommodation at destinations to which they take their passengers. Early examples included Trans World Airlines (Hilton International) and Pan American World

Airways (Inter-Continental Hotels). Although these airlines no longer own hotel chains, they have been succeeded by others, including SAS (see above), All Nippon Airways (Ana Enterprises), Aer Lingus (Copthorne Hotels), Air France (Meridien Hotels), Japan Airlines (Nikko Hotels International), Swissair (Swissôtel), VARIG (Tropical Hotels).

To less developed countries international hotel companies bring management skills and expertise not available locally and help in opening up international markets. For developed countries international hotel operations offer opportunities for the export of skills and expertise, as well as of various goods and services.

Leading international hotel groups are shown in Appendix F. The 50 groups with more than 2.5 million rooms account for around 20 per cent of the total worldwide capacity of hotels and similar establishments of 12.25 million rooms (see Appendix C). North America is the base of 20 of the groups (17 of them in the USA), followed by Europe with 18 (including France 5, Spain 4, UK 4), and the Far East with 10 (including Japan with 7).

Companies engaged in international hotel operations face the basic problems of any hotel group – communications, control and costs – discussed in Chapter 14, and these are accentuated by distance, different languages and different currencies involved. There are also other problems specific to them, which are discussed later in this chapter.

In this chapter international hotel operations are described in terms of their distinctive characteristics and approach, with illustrations from Horwath International reports in the early 1990s. Other variations international hotel companies may expect between regions and countries are shown in other chapters in tables based on the same source. Although the reports are not specifically concerned with international groups, they draw to a great extent on data of hotels of such groups, and provide meaningful illustrations of differences between global regions and countries.

- Hospitality Franchise Systems is the leading international hotel group with most rooms and hotels and is the world's largest hotel franchisor.

- Accor has hotels in more countries than any other group.

- Queens Moat Houses is the management company with most hotels.

(Appendix F)

## Products

An indication of the relative importance of hotel products may be
obtained by comparing the composition of hotel revenue in
different regions and countries, as shown in Tables 45 and 46.
Rooms represent the single most important hotel product in all
regions and countries except in Ireland, and in most of them the
three main products account for around 90 per cent or more of the
total revenue. Variations in the shares of particular products in the
total revenue reflect several influences: the range of products
offered, relative prices of the products, and market and operating
conditions of hotels in different regions and countries. For an
international hotel company the data provide important indicators
for product formulation and for its operational policies (Figure 18).

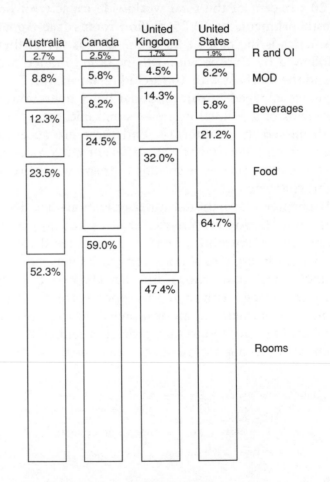

**Figure 18**   Where the Money Came From, 1990

**Table 45**
Composition of Hotel Revenue
in Selected Regions and Countries[a]

|  | Rooms (%) | Food (%) | Beverages (%) | Telephone (%) | Other MOD[b] (%) | R and OI[c] (%) |
|---|---|---|---|---|---|---|
| **Africa and the Middle East** | | | | | | |
| Africa | 48.8 | 32.4 | 8.4 | 5.1 | 2.6 | 2.8 |
| Middle East | 42.3 | 31.5 | 11.3 | 6.2 | 4.3 | 4.5 |
| **Asia and Australia** | | | | | | |
| Asia | 53.6 | 25.4 | 8.9 | 4.0 | 3.0 | 4.1 |
| North Asia | 56.3 | 25.3 | 5.8 | 3.4 | 3.4 | 5.1 |
| Australia | 52.3 | 23.5 | 12.3 | 2.8 | 6.0 | 2.7 |
| **Europe** | | | | | | |
| Continental Europe | 48.4 | 30.8 | 14.2 | 2.6 | 2.3 | 1.5 |
| United Kingdom | 47.4 | 32.0 | 14.3 | 2.2 | 2.3 | 1.7 |
| **North America** | | | | | | |
| Canada | 59.0 | 24.5 | 8.2 | 2.7 | 3.1 | 2.5 |
| United States | 64.7 | 21.2 | 5.8 | 1.9 | 4.3 | 1.9 |
| **Latin America** | | | | | | |
| Mexico | 56.7 | 23.6 | 11.0 | 2.0 | 3.3 | 3.4 |
| South America | 48.1 | 20.6 | 12.2 | 7.3 | 4.0 | 7.0 |

[a]All figures are arithmetic means.
[b]Minor operated departments.
[c]Rentals and other income.
*Source*: Based on *Worldwide Hotel Industry 1991*.

**Table 46**
Composition of Hotel Revenue
in Selected European Countries[a]

|  | Rooms (%) | Food (%) | Beverages (%) | MOD[b] (%) | R and OI[c] (%) |
|---|---|---|---|---|---|
| France | 61.5 | 25.6 | 7.8 | 3.8 | 1.2 |
| Germany | 51.7 | 27.4 | 13.1 | 5.9 | 1.6 |
| Greece | 41.6 | 40.0 | 9.0 | 6.6 | 2.8 |
| Ireland | 31.9 | 37.8 | 25.9 | 3.9 | 0.6 |
| Netherlands | 50.7 | 27.5 | 11.4 | 6.0 | 4.4 |
| Portugal | 58.0 | 24.1 | 8.3 | 7.1 | 1.2 |
| Switzerland | 48.6 | 29.2 | 14.8 | 6.3 | 1.3 |
| United Kingdom | 47.4 | 32.0 | 14.3 | 4.5 | 1.7 |

[a]All figures are arithmetic means.
[b]Minor operated departments.
[c]Rentals and other income.
*Source*: Based on *European Hotel Industry 1991*.

## Markets

Tables 47 and 48 suggest major variations in the extent to which hotels in different regions and countries rely on domestic and foreign guests, and on business, holiday and other markets. In interpreting these figures it is important to bear in mind that they relate mainly to large first class hotels. But for international companies engaged in these markets, the figures provide a simple market segmentation, which is important both in their product formulation and promotion.

**Table 47**
Composition of Hotel Markets
in Selected Regions and Countries[a]

|  | BT (%) | HT (%) | CP (%) | GO (%) | Other (%) |
|---|---|---|---|---|---|
| **Africa and the Middle East** | | | | | |
| Africa | 20 | 60 | 5 | 3 | 12 |
| Middle East | 33 | 24 | 4 | 11 | 28 |
| **Asia and Australia** | | | | | |
| Asia | 30 | 46 | 7 | 7 | 9 |
| North Asia | 32 | 56 | 3 | 1 | 8 |
| Australia | 32 | 46 | 11 | 5 | 6 |
| **Europe** | | | | | |
| Continental Europe | 29 | 50 | 11 | 1 | 9 |
| United Kingdom | 42 | 38 | 15 | 1 | 4 |
| **North America** | | | | | |
| Canada | 31 | 28 | 21 | 11 | 9 |
| United States | 28 | 41 | 20 | 4 | 7 |
| **Latin America** | | | | | |
| Mexico | 20 | 62 | 10 | 3 | 5 |
| South America | 28 | 58 | 6 | 2 | 7 |

[a]All figures are arithmetic means and rounded.
BT, business travellers; HT, holiday tourists; CP, conference participants; GO, government officials.
*Source*: Based on *Worldwide Hotel Industry 1991*.

The great majority of hotel users reserve their accommodation in advance. Table 49 shows the proportions and how the reservations are made in different regions and countries. The operations of international groups account for a high proportion of reservations made through reservations systems and through travel agents and tour operators, both of particular importance in the marketing of international hotels.

**Table 48**
Source of Hotel Business and Composition of Hotel Markets
in Selected European Countries[a]

| | Source of business | | Composition of markets | | | | |
|---|---|---|---|---|---|---|---|
| | Domestic (%) | Foreign (%) | BT (%) | HT (%) | CP (%) | GO (%) | Other (%) |
| France | 42 | 58 | 14 | 61 | 9 | 1 | 15 |
| Germany | 59 | 41 | 41 | 32 | 16 | 2 | 9 |
| Greece | | n.a. | 14 | 68 | 7 | 1 | 10 |
| Ireland | 31 | 69 | 25 | 63 | 6 | 1 | 5 |
| Netherlands | 29 | 71 | 44 | 33 | 12 | – | 11 |
| Portugal | | n.a. | 29 | 53 | 10 | 1 | 8 |
| Switzerland | | n.a. | 35 | 31 | 22 | – | 12 |
| United Kingdom | 63 | 37 | 42 | 38 | 15 | 1 | 4 |

[a]All figures are arithmetic means and rounded.
BT, business travellers; HT, holiday tourists; CP, conference participants; GO, government officials.
*Source*: Based on *European Hotel Industry 1991*.


**Table 49**
Advance Reservations in Hotels
in Selected Regions and Countries[a]

| | Proportion of total | Composition | | | | |
|---|---|---|---|---|---|---|
| | | Direct | Reserv'n system | | TA/TO[b] | Other |
| | | | Own | Ind | | |
| | (%) | (%) | (%) | (%) | (%) | (%) |
| **Africa and the Middle East** | | | | | | |
| Africa | 75.3 | 22.4 | 16.1 | 6.2 | 43.1 | 12.2 |
| Middle East | 83.3 | 33.3 | 24.9 | 2.3 | 25.2 | 14.3 |
| **Asia and Australia** | | | | | | |
| Asia | 79.4 | 25.1 | 18.4 | 7.2 | 39.7 | 8.4 |
| North Asia | 83.7 | 29.1 | 12.6 | 6.1 | 43.9 | 8.3 |
| Australia | 88.4 | 31.9 | 12.5 | 3.0 | 40.2 | 12.4 |
| **Europe** | | | | | | |
| Continental Europe | 90.1 | 44.0 | 9.5 | 5.5 | 32.2 | 8.9 |
| United Kingdom | 92.4 | 46.2 | 16.3 | 4.9 | 23.1 | 9.5 |
| **North America** | | | | | | |
| Canada | 87.1 | 36.8 | 24.3 | 6.3 | 22.9 | 9.7 |
| United States | 81.3 | 49.7 | 18.2 | 4.0 | 18.7 | 9.4 |
| **Latin America** | | | | | | |
| Mexico | 74.9 | 17.6 | 26.9 | 3.9 | 40.7 | 11.0 |
| South America | 85.6 | 22.8 | 9.4 | 6.0 | 56.5 | 5.4 |

[a]All figures are arithmetic means.
[b]Travel agents and tour operators.
*Source*: Based on *Worldwide Hotel Industry 1991*.

As shown in Table 50, with the exception of hotels in the Middle East, only a minority of guests settle their accounts in cash; credit cards and other forms of credit tend to predominate in other regions and countries. Credit cards account for the highest proportion of sales in hotels in North America, other forms of credit in Africa.

**Table 50**
Methods of Payment for Hotel Services
in Selected Regions and Countries[a]

|  | Cash (%) | Credit card (%) | Other credit (%) |
|---|---|---|---|
| **Africa and the Middle East** | | | |
| Africa | 30.6 | 22.2 | 47.3 |
| Middle East | 43.5 | 21.6 | 34.9 |
| **Asia and Australia** | | | |
| Asia | 29.7 | 35.1 | 35.2 |
| North Asia | 32.1 | 38.4 | 29.5 |
| Australia | 33.6 | 34.4 | 32.0 |
| **Europe** | | | |
| Continental Europe | 32.0 | 35.7 | 32.3 |
| United Kingdom | 30.7 | 35.5 | 33.9 |
| **North America** | | | |
| Canada | 21.4 | 51.9 | 26.6 |
| United States | 31.6 | 49.2 | 19.3 |
| **Latin America** | | | |
| Mexico | 25.9 | 45.1 | 29.0 |
| South America | 28.5 | 40.4 | 31.1 |

[a]All figures are arithmetic means.
*Source:* Based on *Worldwide Hotel Industry 1991.*

. . . we see the world as divided into three holiday 'lakes': the Mediterranean, the Caribbean, and the South China Sea. The major markets for tourism are to be found above and below these 'lakes'. They are Western Europe, North America, and Japan/Australia. The orientation of movements in the current phase is vertical – mainly from the north to south. There will also be a second phase, though we have no means of determining the precise moment when it will start – perhaps towards the turn of the century. This phase will witness major lateral movements of tourists from East to West and *vice versa.*

Gilbert Trigano, Club Méditerranée, in *Tourism Management*, Vol. 2, No. 2.

# Ownership and Finance

Many if not most major hotels are not owned by the hotel operator; commonly a separate company is established to own each hotel. Typically each owning company has a major equity investor but there may be also one or more minority equity investors and they may include the hotel operating company. The owning company may seek additional equity investors, if required, grants and soft loans from governments and development agencies, and complete the project financing by raising loans from banks and other commercial sources of finance.

The owning company makes an agreement with the hotel operating company, which may be for:

- a *joint venture* (when the operator is a full partner in the joint ownership of the hotel with a joint participation in the financial outcome);
- a *lease* (when the operator takes temporary possession of the hotel for a specified period of time for rent payment);
- a *management contract* (when the operator who may or may not be also an investor manages the hotel for an agreed remuneration);
- a *franchise* (which could mean that the operator takes a franchise from a franchisor).

Various forms of funding by local interests in the country of operation are combined with external 'national' and 'international' financing.

'National' financing of international hotel operations from sources outside the country of operation takes four main forms:

- Operating companies with a head office in a particular country enter into arrangements in other countries, which may include capital investment as explained above. Examples include -
    from the United Kingdom, Forte, Hilton International and Inter-Continental;
    from the USA, Hilton Corporation, Hyatt International, Marriott, Sheraton, Omni and Westin;
    from France, Accor, Club Méditerranée and Société du Louvre;
    from Spain, Husa, Occidental and the Sol Group;
    from Japan, Nikko, Prince and Tokyu.

- Private institutions such as commercial banks in Europe, North America and the Far East invest in hotels abroad. Examples include Barclays and Morgan Grenfell from the UK, Chase Manhattan and Morgan Guarantee from the USA, Société Generale and Banque de Paris et des Pays-Bas from France, Bank of Tokyo and Mitsui Bank from Japan. Funding by private institutions may be covered by a lender government's export credit guarantee.
- Suppliers of goods and services, particularly construction companies, may participate in, or arrange, equity or loan finance for projects abroad in order to secure a substantial contract.
- Public and semi-public institutions are entrusted by governments to make grants and extend credit, usually to developing countries, where the beneficiaries are normally governments but may also be private firms. The Commonwealth Development Corporation channels overseas aid from the UK overseas aid budget to developing countries for a wide range of tourism-related projects including hotels. In France, the Caisse Centrale de Cooperation Économique, a public development bank, allocates part of French overseas aid to various developments including hotels. In Germany, Deutsche Finanzierungsgesellschaft für Beteiligungen in Entwicklungslaendern is involved in financing hotels in association with companies from the European Community.

'International' financing of hotel operations takes place through:

- Multinational companies, which tend to set up separate companies in different countries and acquire a part interest in them.
- Inter-governmental organizations, such as the World Bank Group and some regional development banks, which lend to developing countries. In Europe, in addition to the European Investment Bank, an institution of the European Community, the European Bank for Reconstruction and Development set up in 1990 assists the emerging democracies of Central and Eastern Europe in their transition to market economies.

The experience of several countries during the recession of the early 1990s emphasizes the need for funding to be supportable by trading profits, as past lending against overinflated capital values resulted in many hotels being unable to service their debts

## Organization and General Approach

Each hotel in a particular country operates in its own environment with its own markets and market conditions, operating conditions, customs and practices; against the background of the country's economic, political and social systems; with its own licensing, labour, tax and other laws. These environments may be very different from each other and also from the environment of the head office wherever it may be situated. The problems of an international hotel group are, therefore, potentially and in practice, generated by three sets of factors: by group operation, by differences between countries, and by the need to cope with the differences in the interests of the group as a whole.

An hotel group which operates hotels within one country has a choice as to the extent of centralization to adopt, as discussed in Chapter 14. The laws of particular countries may impose limits on the extent of centralization of an international hotel group, quite apart from considerations of communications, control and costs set by distance, language and currencies.

Different countries may impose different conditions on the funding of hotel projects, import and export of capital, and the remittance of profits. In many countries expatriate employees may be required in the more senior positions but such employment may be regulated by the governments concerned. The import of supplies of goods and services may be subject to foreign exchange regulations. Budgets and accounts may have to be prepared and reported in local currencies and converted into a common currency for the group. Further problems arise from such happenings as fluctuations in exchange rates.

These considerations imply that a high degree of decentralization is normally required to operate an international hotel company successfully. One group of senior executives usually assumes responsibility for the central functions and another group has territorial operational responsibilities, but some central functions may be to a greater or lesser extent delegated to a regional level.

Two charts illustrate the approach of leading international hotel operators (Figures 19 and 20) whose recent data are included in Appendices E and F.

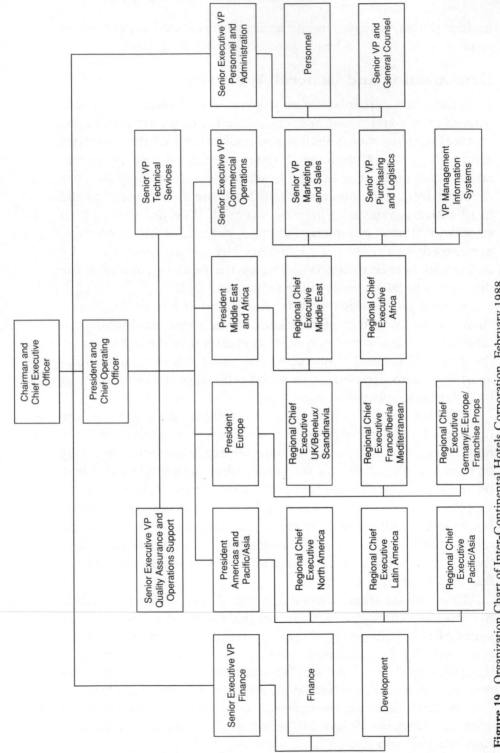

**Figure 19** Organization Chart of Inter-Continental Hotels Corporation, February 1988

Within a decade **Inter-Continental Hotels Corporation** passed from American into British and subsequently (1988) into Japanese ownership. In 1988 it operated only six Inter-Continental and Forum hotels with over 2500 rooms in the UK, but close on a hundred hotels with 37 500 rooms worldwide.

In the preceding year the Company restructured its operations to improve its overhead cost structure, to reduce lines of communications and to identify profit accountability.

Each hotel general manager is accountable to a Regional Chief Executive, who is in turn responsible to a President. Full accountability for profit performance is held in this structure by the Chief Operating Officer, who is also responsible for all sales and marketing worldwide.

Staff functions of finance, marketing and personnel in each of the three regions provide a service to the Regional Presidents, and report on a functional basis to Senior Vice Presidents at the head office.

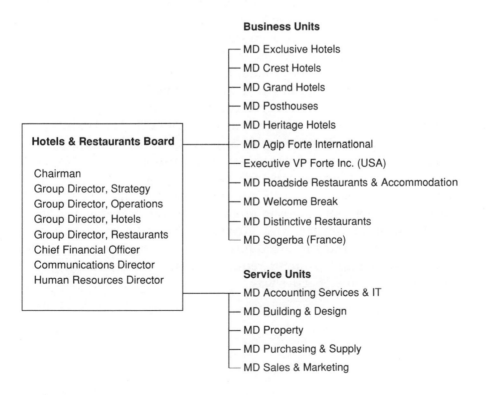

**Figure 20**   Organization Chart of Forte PLC, December 1993

In 1993, **Forte PLC** restructured the company to facilitate a new strategic direction, which was to concentrate on its core business of hotels and restaurants, and to develop internationally.

The divisional format (Hotels, Restaurants, Contract Catering, Airports) was changed to one consisting of a corporate centre and a series of Business Units comprising the company's brands, supported by a number of Service Units (see Figure 20).

The corporate centre (Hotels & Restaurants Board) provides direction and overall control of the business. It is headed by the Chairman who leads a team that covers strategy, finance, communications, human resources and operations (through a main board Operations Director and two other Operations Directors, one focused on hotels and the other on restaurants).

Each Business Unit has a Managing Director (with full supporting team) reporting to an Hotel & Restaurants Board Director. Levels of authority have been increased to enable each Unit to develop its identity, free from the constraints inherent in the old divisional structure. The direction of each Unit is agreed through a strategic planning process, which involves the Business Unit team and the Hotels & Restaurants Board. The size of each Unit ensures that management is close to the action and can pay attention to the quality of product and service delivery, which is an important element in seeking to achieve competitive edge.

The Business Units receive further, tactical, support from specific Service Units (Accounting Services & IT, Building & Design, Property, Purchasing & Supply, Sales & Marketing) and from other group functions such as human resources and communications, whose activities span the group. The remit is to maximize economies of scale for the benefit of all, promote the group as a whole, and to foster cross-selling and inter-unit activity.

The new structure now mirrors the way in which the organization markets its products and has a greater capacity to react to changing consumer requirements, on a brand by brand basis, in a far more effective way.

# Appendices

# Appendix A

**British[a] Hotel Industry[b], 1980–1990**

| | Turnover[c] | | GNP[e] | | Employment[f] | |
|---|---|---|---|---|---|---|
| | at current prices (£m) | at 1990 constant prices[d] (£m) | at current prices (£m) | at 1990 constant prices (£m) | Hotel industry (000) | Total Great Britain (000) |
| 1980 | 2 483 | 4 426 | 231 590 | 422 188 | n.a. | 22 432 |
| 1981 | 2 752 | 4 410 | 256 178 | 419 183 | n.a. | 21 362 |
| 1982 | 2 880 | 4 248 | 280 501 | 426 585 | 229 | 20 896 |
| 1983 | 2 986 | 4 200 | 307 286 | 444 040 | 221 | 20 557 |
| 1984 | 3 374 | 4 523 | 330 196 | 455 980 | 230 | 20 731 |
| 1985 | 4 050 | 5 153 | 359 640 | 469 976 | 234 | 20 910 |
| 1986 | 4 279 | 5 237 | 389 465 | 493 294 | 238 | 20 876 |
| 1987 | 4 781 | 5 612 | 427 138 | 515 720 | 231 | 21 081 |
| 1988 | 5 514 | 6 161 | 475 854 | 542 087 | 245 | 21 748 |
| 1989 | 5 892 | 6 215 | 519 345 | 552 440 | 263 | 22 143 |
| 1990 | 6 370 | 6 370 | 552 748 | 552 748 | 283 | 22 370 |

[a] Refers to Great Britain, i.e. England, Scotland and Wales, excluding Northern Ireland, the Channel Islands and Isle of Man.
[b] Hotels and other residential establishments, i.e. hotels, motels and guest houses providing overnight furnished accommodation with food service, excluding other tourist or short-stay accommodation. Coverage equals VAT trade code 8841 and SIC 1980 Group 665.
[c] Gross takings or total sales and receipts of the businesses on current account inclusive of VAT. The number of businesses, i.e. legal units (companies, partnerships or sole proprietorships) covered decreased year by year from 14 281 in 1980 to 12 767 in 1985 and then rose again gradually to 14 444 in 1990.
[d] Deflated by price index for consumers' expenditure.
[e] Gross National Product at market prices.
[f] Employees in employment at June each year, excluding self-employed. Numbers for 1980 and 1981 not available on a comparable basis to subsequent years because of revision to Standard Industrial Classification.

*Sources*: *Business Monitor SDA28 Catering and Allied Trades* for turnover; *CSO Blue Book 1993* for GNP and price index for consumers' expenditure; *Employment Gazette* for employment.

# Appendix B

**US Hotel Industry[a], 1980–1990**

| | Business receipts[b] | | GNP[c] | | Employment | |
|---|---|---|---|---|---|---|
| | at current prices ($m) | at 1982 constant prices ($m) | at current prices ($bn) | at 1982 constant prices ($bn) | Hotel industry[d] (000) | Total United States (000) |
| 1980 | 26 832 | 31 653 | 2 732.0 | 3 187.1 | 1 038 | 90 406 |
| 1981 | 31 572 | 33 702 | 3 052.6 | 3 248.8 | 1 076 | 91 156 |
| 1982 | 32 749 | 32 749 | 3 166.0 | 3 166.0 | 1 093 | 89 566 |
| 1983 | 35 897 | 34 603 | 3 405.7 | 3 279.1 | 1 131 | 90 200 |
| 1984 | 38 917 | 34 994 | 3 772.2 | 3 501.4 | 1 221 | 94 496 |
| 1985 | 41 837 | 36 038 | 4 014.9 | 3 618.7 | 1 290 | 97 519 |
| 1986 | 43 300 | 35 963 | 4 231.6 | 3 717.9 | 1 338 | 99 525 |
| 1987 | 48 200 | 38 560 | 4 515.6 | 3 853.7 | 1 427 | 102 200 |
| 1988 | 52 400 | 40 342 | 4 873.7 | 4 024.4 | 1 505 | 105 536 |
| 1989 | 58 138 | 43 049 | 5 200.8 | 4 144.1 | 1 549 | 108 413 |
| 1990 | 60 490 | 43 041 | 5 465.1 | 4 227.0 | 1 595 | 109 971 |

[a] Establishments with payroll enumerated under the Standard Industrial Classification Code 7011, hotel/motel, i.e. hotels, motels, motor hotels and tourist courts. According to the quinquennial Census of Service Industries, there were 35 560 such establishments in 1982 and 34 950 in 1987.
[b] Business receipts include guest room rentals, meals, beverages, merchandise and miscellaneous other sales.
[c] Gross National Product.
[d] Payroll employment, i.e. full-time and part-time employees on the payroll of establishments.

*Source*: US Travel Data Center, *The 1990–91 Economic Review of Travel in America*.

# Appendix C

**Global Capacity of Hotels and Similar Establishments[a], 1990**

| Capacities in global regions | Rooms | | Beds | |
|---|---|---|---|---|
| | *Number (000)* | *% of world* | *Number (000)* | *% of world* |
| Europe | 6 333 | 51.7 | 10 339 | 46.1 |
| Americas | 4 096 | 33.4 | 8 207 | 36.6 |
| East Asia and the Pacific (EAP) | 1 200 | 9.8 | 2 613 | 11.7 |
| Africa | 327 | 2.7 | 641 | 2.9 |
| Middle East | 173 | 1.4 | 365 | 1.6 |
| Southern Asia | 120 | 1.0 | 241 | 1.1 |
| World | 12 249 | 100.0 | 22 406 | 100.0 |

| Major capacities in Europe | *Number (000)* | *% of Europe* | *Number (000)* | *% of Europe* |
|---|---|---|---|---|
| Italy | 938 | 14.8 | 1 704 | 16.5 |
| Germany | | n.a. | 1 110 | 10.7 |
| Spain | 603 | 9.5 | 1 102 | 10.7 |
| France (1989) | 544 | 8.6 | 1 088 | 10.5 |
| United Kingdom | | n.a. | 994 | 9.6 |

| Major capacities in the Americas | *Number (000)* | *% of Americas* | *Number (000)* | *% of Americas* |
|---|---|---|---|---|
| United States | 3 033 | 74.0 | 5459 | 66.5 |
| Mexico | 334 | 8.2 | 667 | 8.1 |

| Major capacities in East Asia and the Pacific (EAP) | *Number (000)* | *% of EAP* | *Number (000)* | *% of EAP* |
|---|---|---|---|---|
| China | 294 | 24.5 | 634 | 24.3 |
| Japan | 212 | 17.7 | n.a. | |
| Thailand | 169 | 14.1 | n.a. | |
| Australia | 157 | 13.1 | 451 | 17.3 |

[a] For most countries, hotels and similar establishments include hotels, motels, inns and boarding houses, but only classified hotels for France; figures for the United Kingdom refer to England only.

*Source*: World Tourism Organization, *Compendium of Tourism Statistics 1986–1990*.

# Appendix D

**Average Annual Rates of Hotel Occupancy[a]**
**in Selected OECD Member Countries, 1989, 1990, 1991**

|  | 1989 (%) | 1990 (%) | 1991 (%) |
|---|---|---|---|
| *Bed occupancy* | | | |
| Australia | 32.6 | 31.7 | 30.9 |
| Austria | n.a. | 29.8 | 31.9 |
| Belgium | 29.9 | 30.7 | n.a. |
| Germany | 40.0 | 42.2 | 43.5 |
| Italy | 38.2 | 39.2 | 39.1 |
| Netherlands | 22.3 | 25.1 | 23.7 |
| Norway | 35.9 | 34.5 | 35.3 |
| Portugal | 50.8 | 51.4 | n.a. |
| Spain | 52.7 | n.a. | 51.3 |
| Sweden | 32.5 | 30.7 | 26.4 |
| Switzerland | 35.7 | 36.4 | 36.2 |
| Turkey | 44.5 | 45.1 | 35.4 |
| United Kingdom | 44.9 | 45.8 | n.a. |
| *Room occupancy* | | | |
| Finland | 52.1 | 48.4 | 42.9 |
| Japan | 74.7 | 77.6 | 75.9 |

[a] Occupancy rates registered in hotels only unless stated otherwise (derived as arithmetic average of monthly occupancy rates):

| | |
|---|---|
| Australia | Hotels and motels with facilities |
| Austria | Registered hotels; 1991 based on first 10 months |
| Finland | Hotels and similar establishments |
| Germany | Registered accommodation with 9 or more beds |
| Japan | Member hotels of Japan Hotel Association |
| Netherlands | All means of accommodation |
| Norway | Registered accommodation with 20 or more beds |
| Portugal | Hotels, studio-hotels, motels and state-owned inns |
| Sweden | Hotels, motels, holiday villages and youth hostels |
| Switzerland | Hotels, motels and inns |
| Turkey | Hotels, motels, boarding houses, inns, holiday villages |
| United Kingdom | Figures apply to England only |

*Source*: Based on OECD, *Tourism Policy and International Tourism*.

# Appendix E

## Leading Hotel Groups in Britain

| | | Rooms | Hotels | Notes |
|---|---|---|---|---|
| 1 | Forte | 30 343 | 344 | See also App. F no. 8 |
| 2 | Mount Charlotte Thistle Hotels | 14 071 | 109 | Parent co.: Brierley Investments, Wellington |
| 3 | Queens Moat Houses | 10 407 | 102 | See also App. F no. 30 |
| 4 | Hilton UK | 8 501 | 40 | See also App. F nos. 7, 13 |
| 5 | Whitbread Group of Hotels | 4 438 | 94 | Travel Inns, Lansbury and Country Club Hotels |
| 6 | Swallow Hotels | 4 397 | 35 | Parent co.: Vaux Group PLC, Sunderland |
| 7 | Accor UK | 4 120 | 28 | See also App. F no. 3 |
| 8 | Holiday Inn Worldwide | 4 052 | 23 | See also App. F no. 2 |
| 9 | Stakis Hotels | 3 688 | 30 | Parent co.: Stakis PLC, Glasgow |
| 10 | Jarvis Hotels | 3 522 | 43 | Formerly Embassy Hotels |
| 11 | Marriott Hotels | 3 225 | 17 | See also App. F no. 5 |
| 12 | Imperial London Hotels | 3 046 | 7 | Private company |
| 13 | De Vere Hotels | 2 703 | 22 | Parent co.: Greenalls Group, Warrington |
| 14 | Coast & Country Hotels | 2 650 | 31 | |
| 15 | Copthorne Hotels | 2 568 | 12 | Parent co.: Aer Lingus |
| 16 | Resort Hotels | 2 462 | 49 | Includes Penguin Hotel Group |
| 17 | Rank Hotels | 2 434 | 18 | Parent co.: The Rank Organisation, see also no. 27 |
| 18 | Metropole Hotels | 2 280 | 5 | Parent co.: Lonrho PLC, London |
| 19 | Friendly Hotels | 2 134 | 20 | |
| 20 | Edwardian Hotels | 1 862 | 9 | |
| 21 | Principal Hotels | 1 750 | 19 | |
| 22 | Inter-Continental Hotels | 1 717 | 5 | See also no. 35 below and App. F no. 15 |
| 23 | North British Trust Hotels | 1 503 | 18 | |

| | Rooms | Hotels | Notes |
|---|---|---|---|
| 24 Toby Hotels | 1 457 | 45 | Parent co.: Bass PLC, London |
| 25 ITT Sheraton | 1 439 | 5 | See also App. F no. 6 |
| 26 Britannia Hotels | 1 320 | 6 | |
| 27 Butlin's Holiday Hotels | 1 313 | 5 | Parent co.: The Rank Organisation, see also no. 17 |
| 28 Ramada International | 1 294 | 4 | See also App. F no. 17 |
| 29 Chef & Brewer Inns | 1 066 | 47 | Parent co.: Scottish and Newcastle |
| 30 Firoka Group | 1 061 | 10 | |
| 31 Sarova Hotels | 1 007 | 6 | |
| 32 Scandic Crown Hotels | 995 | 4 | See also App. F no. 27 |
| 33 Park Hotels (GB) | 982 | 8 | |
| 34 Belhaven Hotels | 945 | 10 | |
| 35 Forum Hotels | 910 | 1 | See also no. 22 above and App. F no. 15 |
| 36 Granada Lodges | 875 | 21 | |
| 37 CG Hotels | 872 | 6 | |
| 38 Periquito Hotels | 860 | 10 | |
| 39 Seymour Hotels | 838 | 5 | Channel Islands |
| 40 Campanile UK | 830 | 14 | See also App. F no. 19 |
| 41 Oriel Leisure Hotels | 794 | 10 | |
| 42 Compass Hotels | 782 | 11 | |
| 43 Park Inns International | 736 | 2 | See also App. F no. 36 |
| 44 Muirgold | 710 | 5 | |
| 45 Savoy Group | 704 | 5 | |
| 46 Leisureplex Hotels | 703 | 9 | |
| 47 Premier House | 634 | 22 | |
| 48 Hyatt Hotels & Resorts | 621 | 3 | See also App. F no. 9 |
| 49 Brend Hotel Group | 612 | 10 | |
| 50 Sovereign Hotel Group London | 580 | 3 | |

*Source*: Based on *Caterer & Hotelkeeper*, 10 June 1993.

*Appendix F*

**Leading International Hotel Groups**

| | | Rooms[a] | Hotels | Countries | Head Office | Notes |
|---|---|---|---|---|---|---|
| 1 | Hospitality Franchise Systems | 354 997 | 3413[b] | 7[c] | Parsippany, NJ, USA | Howard Johnson, HoJo Inns, Days Inns, Super 8 plus Ramada Hotels in USA. Parent co.: Blackstone Group, New York |
| 2 | Holiday Inn Worldwide | 328 679 | 1692[b] | 55[c] | Atlanta, GA, USA | Crowne Plaza, Express, Garden Court. Parent co.: Bass PLC, London |
| 3 | Accor | 238 990 | 2098 | 66 | Evry, France | Altea, Compris, Formule 1, Hotelia, Ibis, Mercure, Motel 6, Novotel, PanSea, PLM Azur, Pullman, Sofitel, Urbis |
| 4 | Choice Hotels International | 230 430 | 2502[b] | 27 | Silver Spring, MD, USA | Clarion, Comfort, Quality, Rodeway, Sleep Inn. Parent co.: Manor Care |
| 5 | Marriott | 166 919 | 750 | 20 | Washington, DC, USA | Marriott Hotels & Resorts, Courtyard Inn, Fairfield Inn, Residence Inn |
| 6 | ITT Sheraton | 132 361 | 426[b] | 61 | Boston, MA, USA | Parent co.: ITT Corporation, New York |
| 7 | Hilton Hotels Corporation | 94 653 | 242[b] | 5[c] | Beverley Hills, CA, USA | Includes Conrad Hotels, firm's non-USA brand |
| 8 | Forte | 79 309 | 871 | 33 | London, UK | 46% Travelodge brand in USA, 45% various brands in Europe |
| 9 | Hyatt Hotels/Hyatt Intnl | 77 579 | 164 | 37[c] | Chicago, IL, USA | 59 hotels/21 079 rooms international, remainder domestic. Parent co.: Pritzker Family Trust, Chicago |

| | | Rooms[a] | Hotels | Countries | Head Office | Notes |
|---|---|---|---|---|---|---|
| 10 | Carlson/Radisson/Colony | 76 069 | 336[b] | 30 | Minneapolis, MN, USA | Mainly Radisson, also Colony Hotels & Resorts and Country Lodging. Parent co.: Carlson, Minneapolis |
| 11 | Promus | 75 558 | 459[b] | 2[c] | Memphis, TN, USA | Harrah's (casino hotels), Embassy Suites, Hampton Inns, Homewood Suites |
| 12 | Club Méditerranée | 63 067 | 261 | 32 | Paris, France | Club Med, Maeva, Aquarius, Valtur and City Club |
| 13 | Hilton International | 52 979 | 160 | 47 | Watford, Herts., UK | Includes Vista (US brand), Hilton National or Associate. Parent co.: Ladbroke Group PLC, Watford |
| 14 | Sol Group | 40 163 | 156 | 16[c] | Palma de Mallorca, Spain | Mélia and Sol Hotels |
| 15 | Inter-Continental Hotels | 39 000 | 104 | 47 | London, UK | 87 Inter-Continental and 17 Forum hotels. Parent co.: Saison Group, Tokyo |
| 16 | Westin Hotels & Resorts | 38 029 | 75 | 15[c] | Seattle, WA, USA | Parent co.: Aoki Corporation, Tokyo |
| 17 | New World/Ramada Intnl | 36 520 | 133 | 43 | Hong Kong | 122 Ramada and 11 New World Hotels |
| 18 | Canadian Pacific Hotels | 27 970 | 86 | 2 | Toronto, Ontario, Canada | Canadian Pacific Hotels & Resorts and Doubletree Hotels |
| 19 | Société du Louvre | 27 427 | 398 | 6[c] | Paris, France | Campanile, Concorde, Premiere Class, Bleu Marine |
| 20 | Tokyu Hotel Group | 22 671 | 102 | 11 | Tokyo, Japan | Tokyu Inns, Tokyu Hotels, Pan Pacific hotels and resorts and smaller brands |

| | | Rooms[a] | Hotels | Countries | Head Office | Notes |
|---|---|---|---|---|---|---|
| 21 | Hospitality International | 22 425 | 345[b] | 3 | Tucker, GA, USA | Scottish Inns, Red Carpet Inns, Master Host Inns, Downtowner, Passport Inns |
| 22 | Husa Hotels Group | 21 500 | 98 | 3 | Barcelona, Spain | Husa, Hogama, Entursa, Lihsa hotels |
| 23 | Prince Hotels | 20 249 | 70 | 6 | Tokyo, Japan | Parent co.: Seibu, Tokyo |
| 24 | Meridien Hotels | 18 261 | 58 | 35 | Paris, France | Parent co.: Air France, Paris |
| 25 | Omni Hotels | 18 148 | 45 | 4 | Hampton, NH, USA | Includes Dunfey hotels. Parent co.: The Wharf (Holdings) Ltd, Hong Kong |
| 26 | SAS Intnl Hotels/Sunwing | 16 507 | 46 | 11 | Brussels, Belgium | Parent co.: SAS Stockholm |
| 27 | Scandic Hotels | 16 000 | 97 | 9[c] | Stockholm, Sweden | Parent co.: Förvaltnings AB Ratos, Stockholm |
| 28 | Stouffer Hotels | 15 767 | 41 | 2[c] | Solon, OH, USA | Includes Presidente brand in Mexico. Parent co.: Nestlé |
| 29 | Fujita Kanko | 14 891 | 65 | 2 | Tokyo, Japan | Fujita Hotels, Kowaki-en-Hotels, Washington Hotels |
| 30 | Queens Moat Houses | 14 697 | 126 | 9 | Romford, Essex, UK | |
| 31 | Nikko Hotels International | 13 590 | 33 | 15 | Tokyo, Japan | Parent co.: Japan Airlines, Tokyo |
| 32 | Reso Hotels | 13 350 | 61 | 5[c] | Stockholm, Sweden | Reso and Sara Hotels, Sara Travel & Hotel Group |
| 33 | Southern Pacific Hotels | 12 346 | 70 | 9 | Sydney, Australia | Parkroyal Hotels, Travelodge, THC, Centra. Parent co.: Hale Corporation, Hong Kong, owned by Pritzker Family Trust, Chicago |

| | | Rooms[a] | Hotels | Countries | Head Office | Notes |
|---|---|---|---|---|---|---|
| 34 | Four Season Hotels/Resorts | 11 894 | 34 | 13 | Toronto, Ontario, Canada | Includes Regent Hotels |
| 35 | Ana Enterprises | 11 210 | 33 | 7 | Tokyo, Japan | Parent co.: All Nippon Airways, Tokyo |
| 36 | Park Inns International | 11 006 | 80[b] | 7 | Irving, TX, USA | Includes Park Plaza |
| 37 | Maritim Hotels | 10 900 | 41 | 4 | Bad Salzuflen, Germany | |
| 38 | Shangri-La International | 10 163 | 21 | 9 | Hong Kong | Parent co.: Kuok Group |
| 39 | Wyndham Hotels & Resorts | 9 762 | 37 | 6[c] | Dallas, TX, USA | |
| 40 | Occidental Hotels | 9 468 | 44 | 12 | Madrid, Spain | |
| 41 | Climat de France | 8 989 | 175 | 4[c] | Les Ulis, France | Climat and Nuit D'Hotels |
| 42 | Ritz-Carlton | 8 909 | 27 | 2 | Atlanta, GA, USA | Parent co.: W B Johnson Properties, Atlanta |
| 43 | Sunroute Hotel System | 8 114 | 72[b] | 4 | Tokyo, Japan | |
| 44 | Taj Group of Hotels | 8 000 | 45 | 10 | Bombay, India | Taj Hotels, Garden Retreats, Gateway Hotels/Resorts. Parent co.: Indian Hotel Co Ltd, Bombay |
| 45 | Dai-Ichi Hotels | 7 860 | 42 | 6 | Tokyo, Japan | |
| 46 | Steigenberger Hotels | 7 563 | 44 | 5 | Frankfur/Main, Germany | Steigenberger, Avance, Maxx InterCity, Esprit |
| 47 | Protea Hospitality Corpn | 7 483 | 117[a] | 6 | Capetown, South Africa | Protea and Places Hotels |
| 48 | Delta Hotels & Resorts | 7 072 | 19 | 3 | Toronto, Ontario, Canada | Parent co.: Realston Hotels Limited, Toronto |
| 49 | Fiesta Hotels | 7 000 | 27 | 2[c] | Ibiza, Spain | |
| 50 | Loews Hotels | 6 938 | 14 | 3[c] | New York, NY, USA | |

[a] Rankings are based on hotel rooms open as at 31 December 1992.
[b] All or most hotels franchised.
[c] Most hotels located in country of head office.

Source: Based on *Hotels*, July 1993.

# Appendix G
## Horwath International Reports

Most illustrations of hotel operations in this book draw on *Worldwide Hotel Industry* published by Horwath International. What the reader should be aware of when interpreting the data is described below.

All data originate from Horwath International questionnaires completed by contributing hotels and are subject to non-sampling errors, such as differences in the interpretation of questions by the respondents.

The terminology and definitions follow the 8th revised edition of the *Uniform System of Accounts for Hotels*. An explanation of the main terms and bases used is given in each report but the reader is advised to consult the *Uniform System* for detail.

Arithmetic means of contributing hotels are used for certain parts, but most amounts are medians, i.e. middle values of each series, which do not add to median totals.

Each item is analysed separately and the reported amounts and ratios are calculated for each item, since all hotels do not report information for each item. Footnotes to tables in this book show the basis used in each case.

All amounts are expressed in the common currency of the US dollar, into which amounts in national currencies have been converted, and currency conversion tables used are given in each report. Users of the information should be aware that currency fluctuations may have a significant effect on the dollar values.

Amounts and ratios are examined separately for five global regions and each region is sub-divided into two or three sub-regions or countries, giving data for up to twelve geographical areas.

Data are indicative of contributing hotels but not necessarily representative of any type of hotel or of any region, sub-region or country.

The general profile of the typical contributing hotel in the early 1990s is shown below:

| | |
|---|---|
| *Age* | Post 1980 |
| | Some older in Europe and North America |
| *Size* | 100–300 rooms |
| | Some larger in Asia and Australia |
| | Some smaller in Europe |
| *Location* | Urban, mainly city centre |
| | Some suburban in Europe and North America |
| | Some resort in Asia and Australia, North America, Latin America and Caribbean |
| *Market* | Primarily business travellers and leisure tourists |
| | Also conference participants in North America |
| *Management* | Chain owned/managed/affiliated |
| | Some independent in Europe, North America, Latin America and Caribbean. |

Some illustrations in this book show hotel operations in a number of European countries as reported to European member firms of Horwath International and published annually in *European Hotel Industry*. Most of the foregoing notes relating to *Worldwide Hotel Industry* apply also to this report and the data it includes. To facilitate comparison between countries, amounts are expressed in European Currency Units (ECU), into which original data have been converted; however, currency fluctuations may have a significant effect on the ECU values.

Most statistics refer to the early 1990s, the latest available period, when both in Europe and elsewhere hotel operations were seriously affected by worldwide economic recession. This together with such influences as the Gulf crisis resulted in a general downturn in international travel, and decrease in hotel occupancies and room rates, especially in Europe, North America and Latin America.

# Appendix H
## Select List of Hotel and Related Organizations

### Australia
Australian Hotels Association
8 Quay Street, Sydney, NSW 2000

Catering Institute of Australia
PO Box 388, Pennant Hills, Sydney, NSW 2120

### Canada
The Hotel Association of Canada Inc.
Suite 1505, 155 Carlton Street, Winnipeg, Manitoba R3C 3H8

Canadian Hospitality Federation
Suite 102, 2200 Lake Shore Blvd West, Toronto, Ontario M8V 1A4

### Ireland
Council for Education, Recruitment and Training (CERT)
CERT House, Amiens Street, Dublin 1

Irish Hotels Federation
13 Northbrook Road, Ranelagh, Dublin 6

### New Zealand
Hotel Association of New Zealand
8th Floor, Education House, 178 Willis Street, Wellington

### South Africa
Federated Hotel Association of South Africa
PO Box 514, Rivonia 2128

# United Kingdom
British Hospitality Association
40 Duke Street, London W1M 6HR

Hotel, Catering & Institutional Management Association
191 Trinity Road, London SW17 7HN

# United States
American Hotel & Motel Association
1201 New York Avenue NW, Suite 600, Washington DC 20005

International Council on Hotel, Restaurant and Institutional
Education (CHRIE)
1200 17th Street NW, Washington, DC 20036-3097

# International
ASEAN Hotel and Restaurant Association (AHRA)
c/o Bank Pacific, 4th Floor, Jalan Jenderal Sudirman 8, Jakarta,
Indonesia (brings together hotel and restaurant groups in
Indonesia, Malaysia, Philippines, Singapore and Thailand)

Caribbean Hotel Association (CHA)
18 Marseilles St, Ste 2B, Santurce 00907, Puerto Rico

Confederation of National Hotel and Restaurant Associations in
the European Community (HOTREC)
Bd Anspach 111, Bte 4, B-1000 Brussels, Belgium

Inter-American Hotel Association (IAHA)
Fernandez Albano 171, 3er Piso, Casilla 3410, Santiago, Chile

International Association of Hotel Management Schools (IAHMS)
c/o Hague Hotel School, Brusselselaan 2, B-2587 AH Den Haag,
Netherlands

International Association of Hotel School Directors
Euhofa International, Le Chalet-à-Gobet, CH-1000 Lausanne 25,
Switzerland

International Hotel Association (IHA)
80 rue de la Roquette, F-75544 Paris Cedex 11, France

International Hotel Association South Asia (IHASA)
PO 2151, Tripureswar, Kathmandu, Nepal

International Organization of Hotel and Restaurant Associations
(HoReCa)
Blumenfeldstrasse 20, CH-8046 Zurich, Switzerland

Nordic Hotel and Restaurant Association
c/o SHR, Box 1158, S-111 81 Stockholm, Sweden (brings together hotel and restaurant associations in Denmark, Finland, Iceland, Norway and Sweden)

# Appendix I
## Select List of Hotel Periodicals

## United Kingdom

*Caterer & Hotelkeeper* (weekly)
Reed Business Publishing Ltd, Quadrant House, The Quadrant, Sutton, Surrey SM2 5AS

*Hospitality* (bimonthly)
Hotel, Catering and Institutional Management Association (HCIMA), 191 Trinity Road, London SW17 7HN

*Hotel Management* (monthly)
Quantum Publishing Ltd, 29–31 Lower Coombe Street, Croydon CR9 1LX

*International Journal of Contemporary Hospitality Management*
MCB University Press Ltd, 60/62 Toller Lane, Bradford, West Yorks BD8 9BY

*International Journal of Hospitality Management* (quarterly)
Elsevier Science Ltd, The Boulevard, Langford Lane, Kidlington, Oxford OX5 1GB

*Voice of the British Hospitality Association* (BHA, monthly)
40 Duke Street, London W1M 6HR

## United States

*Cornell Hotel & Restaurant Administration Quarterly* (bimonthly)
Cornell Hotel School, 255 Statler Hall, Cornell University, Ithaca, NY 14853-0223

*Hospitality and Tourism Educator*
Department of Nutrition and Food Science, San Jose State University, 1 Washington Square, San Jose, CA 95192-0058

*Hospitality Research Journal* (3x annually)
International Council on Hotel, Restaurant and Institutional Education (CHRIE), 1200 17th Street NW, Washington, DC 20036-3097

*Hotel & Motel Management* (2x a month except monthly in January, August and December)
Advanstar Communications Inc, 7500 Old Oak Boulevard, Cleveland, OH 44130

*Hotels* (monthly)
Cahners Publishing Co, 1350 East Touhy Avenue, Des Plaines, IL 60017

*Lodging Hospitality* (monthly)
Penton Publishing Inc, 1100 Superior Avenue, Cleveland, OH 44114

## Other Countries

*Australian Hotelier* (monthly)
Official Magazine of the Australian Hotels Association (AHA)
The National Publishing Group in conjunction with AHA, Level 2, 44 Chippen Street, Chippendale, NSW 2008, Australia

*Canadian Hotel and Restaurant* (monthly)
Maclean Hunter Ltd, Maclean Hunter Buildings, 777 Bay Street, Toronto, Canada MSW 1A7

*Catering and Accommodation Management* (monthly)
Trade Publications Ltd, 13 Cheshire Street, Parnell, Auckland, New Zealand

*Hotel & Catering Review* (monthly)
Jemma Publications Ltd, 22 Brookfield Avenue, Blackrock, Co Dublin, Eire

*Hotelier & Caterer* (monthly)
Uitvlug, Howard Drive, Pinelands 7405, Cape Town, South Africa

# Appendix J
# Suggested Further Reading

## Chapter 1   Staying Away from Home
Burkart A. J. and Medlik S., *Tourism – Past, Present and Future*, Part I
Fenton L., Fowler N. A. and Parkinson G. S., *Hotel Accounts and Their Audit*, Chapter 1
Jones P. and Lockwood A., *The Management of Hotel Operations*, Chapter 1
Odgers P., *The Hotel, Catering and Leisure Industry*
Quest M., ed., *Horwath Book of Tourism*, Chapters 1, 16, 17

## Chapter 2   Hotel Products and Markets
Buttle F., *Hotel and Food Service Marketing*, Chapters 4, 5, 6
Doswell, R., *Towards an Integrated Approach to Hotel Planning*, Part 1
Greene, M., *Marketing Hotels and Restaurants into the 90s*, Chapters 5, 7
Lockwood A. and Jones P., *People and the Hotel and Catering Industry*, Chapter 11
Venison P., *Managing Hotels*, Chapter 16

## Chapter 3   Hotel Policies, Philosophies and Strategies
Boella M. J., *Human Resource Management in the Hospitality Industry*, Chapter 2
Buttle F., *Hotel and Food Service Marketing*, Chapter 7
Gullen H. V., and Rhodes G. E., *Management in the Hotel and Catering Industry*, Chapters 1–4
Hornsey T. and Dann D., *Manpower Management in the Hotel and Catering Industry*, Chapter 2
Jones P. and Lockwood A., *The Management of Hotel Operations*, Chapter 2
Teare R. *et al*, eds, *Managing and Marketing Services into the 1990s*
Teare R. *et al*, eds, *Managing Projects in Hospitality Organizations*
Teare R. and Boer A., eds, *Strategic Hospitality Management*
Venison P., *Managing Hotels*, Chapter 9
Witt S. F., Brooke M. Z. and Buckley P. J., *The Management of International Tourism*, Chapter 9

## Chapter 4   Rooms and Beds
Abbott P. and Lewry S., *Front Office*
Allen D., *Accommodation and Cleaning Services*, Volume 2

Braham, B., *Hotel Front Office*
Branson J. C. and Lennox M., *Hotel, Hostel and Hospital Housekeeping*
Dix C. and Baird C., *Front Office Operations*
Fellows J., *Housekeeping Supervision*
Hatfield D. and Winter C., *Professional Housekeeping*
Hotel and Catering Training Company, *The Accommodation Operation*
Hotel and Catering Training Company, *Accommodation Operations*
Hotel and Catering Training Company, *Front of House Operation*
Hotel and Catering Training Company, *Maximising Occupancy*
Hurst R., *Accommodation Management*
Jones C. and Paul V., *Accommodation Management*
Paige G. and J., *The Hotel Receptionist*
White P. B and Beckley H., *Hotel Reception*

## Chapter 5   Food and Drink

Anderson C. and Blakemore D., *Modern Food Service*
Andrioli S. and Douglas P., *Professional Food Service*
Davis B. and Stone S., *Food and Beverage Management*
Fuller J. and Kirk D., *Kitchen Planning and Management*
Fuller J. and Waller K., *The Menu, Food and Profit*
Julyan B., *Beverage Sales and Service*
Kinton R., Ceserani V. and Foskett D., *The Theory of Catering*
Lillicrap D. R. and Cousins J. A., *Food and Beverage Service*
Odgers P., *Purchasing, Costing and Control for Hotel and Catering Operations*
Wood F. and Lightowlers P., *Purchasing, Costing and Control in the Hotel and Catering Industry*

## Chapter 6   Miscellaneous Guest Services

Braham B., *Hotel Front Office*, Chapter 6
Dix C. and Baird C., *Front Office Operations*, Chapter 1
White P. B. and Beckley H., *Hotel Reception*, Chapters 10 and 11

## Chapter 7   Hotel Organization

Boella M. J., *Human Resource Management in the Hospitality Industry*, Chapter 18
Fenton L., Fowler N. A. and Parkinson G. S., *Hotel Accounts and Their Audit*, Chapter 2
Gullen H. V. and Rhodes G. E., *Management in the Hotel and Catering Industry*, Chapters 5, 6
Hornsey T. and Dann D., *Manpower Management in the Hotel and Catering Industry*, passim
Lockwood A. and Jones P., *People and the Hotel and Catering Industry*, Chapter 10
Teare R. *et al*, eds, *Managing and Marketing Services into the 1990s*
Teare R. *et al*, eds, *Managing Projects in Hospitality Organizations*
Teare R. and Boer A., eds, *Strategic Hospitality Management*
Venison P., *Managing Hotels*, Chapter 8
Wood R. C. *Working in Hotels and Catering*

## Chapter 8   Hotel Staffing

Boella M. J., *Human Resource Management in the Hospitality Industry*
Gale K., *Behavioural and Supervisory Studies for Hotel and Catering Operations*
Goss-Turner S., *Managing People in the Hotel and Catering Industry*
Hornsey T. and Dann D., *Manpower Management in the Hotel and Catering Industry*

Hotel and Catering Training Company, *Employee Relations*
Jones P. and Lockwood A., *The Management of Hotel Operations*, Chapter 4
Lockwood A. and Jones P., *People and the Hotel and Catering Industry*
Mullins L., *Hospitality Management. A Human Resources Approach*
Riley M., *Human Resource Management*
Venison P., *Managing Hotels*, Chapter 5, 6, 7, 15
Wood R. C., *Working in Hotels and Catering*

## Chapter 9 Productivity in Hotels

Boella M. J., *Human Resource Management in the Hospitality Industry*, Chapter 19
Braham B., *Computer Systems in the Hotel and Catering Industry*
Cunningham S., *Data Analysis in Hotel and Catering Management*
Fenton L., Fowler N. A. and Parkinson G. S., *Hotel Accounts and Their Audit*, Chapter 12
Gamble P., *Small Computers and Hospitality Management*
Godowski S., *Microcomputers in the Hotel and Catering Industry*
Gullen H. V. and Rhodes G. E., *Management in the Hotel and Catering Industry*, Chapter 9
Johnson K. and Ball S., *Productivity Measurement in Hotels*. In *Tourism Marketing and Management Handbook* (S. F. Witt and L. Moutinho, eds.)
Jones C. and Paul V., *Accommodation Management*, Chapter 3
Jones P. and Lockwood A., *The Management of Hotel Operations*, Chapter 8
Medlik S., ed., *Managing Tourism*, Chapters 23, 24
Medlik S., *Tourism and Productivity*
National Economic Development Committee, *Costs and Manpower Productivity in UK Hotels*
Smith J., *Practical Computing*
Teare R. and Boer A., eds, *Strategic Hospitality Management*, Chapter 4

## Chapter 10 Marketing

Abbott P. and Lewry S., *Front Office*, Chapters 7, 8, 10
Buttle F., *Hotel and Food Service Marketing*
Fewell A. and Wills N., *Marketing*
Greene M., *Marketing Hotels and Restaurants into the 90s*
Hotel and Catering Training Board, *Marketing for Hotels and Restaurants*
Hotel and Catering Training Company, *Maximising Occupancy*
Jones P. and Lockwood A., *The Management of Hotel Operations*, Chapters 5, 9
Lockwood A. and Jones P., *People and the Hotel and Catering Industry*, Chapter 11
Middleton V. T. C., *Marketing in Travel and Tourism*, Chapter 23
Roberts J., *Marketing for the Hospitality Industry*
Shepherd J. W., *Marketing Practice in the Hotel and Catering Industry*
Taylor D., *Hotel and Catering Sales*
Teare R. *et al*, eds, *Managing and Marketing Services into the 1990s*, Part IV
Venison P., *Managing Hotels*, Chapter 16
Ward T. J., *The Hotel Feasibility Study – Principles and Practice*. In *Progress in Tourism, Recreation and Hospitality Management* Vol 1 (C. P. Cooper, ed.)

## Chapter 11 Property Ownership and Management

Fellows R. and J., *Buildings for Hospitality*
Gladwell D. C., *Practical Maintenance and Equipment*
Hurst R., *Accommodation Management*, Chapters 2, 3, 6
International Hotels Environment Initiative, *Environmental Management for Hotels*
Jones C. and Paul V., *Accommodation Management*, Chapters 1, 2
Jones P. and Lockwood A., *The Management of Hotel Operations*, Chapter 3

## Chapter 12   Finance and Accounts

Boardman R. D., *Hotel and Catering Accounts*
Fenton L., Fowler N. A. and Parkinson G. S., *Hotels Accounts and Their Audit*
Harris, P., *Profit Planning*
Harris P. and Hazzard P., *Accounting in the Hotel and Catering Industry*
Harris P. and Hazzard P., *Managerial Accounting in the Hotel and Catering Industry*
International Association of Hospitality Accountants, *Uniform System of Accounts for Hotels*
Kotas R., *Accounting in the Hotel and Catering Industry*
Kotas R., *Management Accounting for Hotels and Restaurants*
Messenger S. and Shaw H., *Financial Management for the Hospitality, Tourism and Leisure Industries*
Sutton D. F., *Financial Management in Hotel and Catering Operations*
Walton P., *Modern Financial Accounting in the Hospitality Industry*
Wood F. and Lightowlers P., *Accounting in the Hotel and Catering Industry*

## Chapter 13   The Small Hotel

Fenton L., Fowler N. A. and Parkinson G. S., *Hotel Accounts and Their Audit*, Chapter 13
Hotel and Catering Training Board, *Starting Up Your Own Business in the Hotel and Catering Industry*
Lennick J., *Running Your Own Small Hotel*
Quest M., *How to Buy Your Own Hotel*

## Chapter 14   Hotel Groups

Fenton L., Fowler N. A. and Parkinson G. S., *Hotel Accounts and Their Audit*, Chapter 9

## Chapter 15   International Hotel Operations

Fenton L., Fowler N. A. and Parkinson G. S., *Hotel Accounts and Their Audit*, Chapter 10
Gliatis N. and Guerrier Y., *Managing International Career Moves in International Hotel Companies.* In *Progress in Tourism, Recreation and Hospitality Management*, Vol 5 (C. P. Cooper and A. Lockwood, eds)
Hodgson A., *The Travel and Tourism Industry*, Chapter 8
Hornsey T. and Dann D., *Manpower Management in the Hotel and Catering Industry*, Chapter 10
Jones P. and Pizam A., eds, *The International Hospitality Industry*
McQueen, M., *Multinationals in Tourism.* In *Tourism Marketing and Management Handbook* (S. F. Witt and L. Moutinho, eds)
Quest M., ed, *Horwath Book of Tourism*, Chapter 17
Teare R. and Boer R., eds, *Strategic Hospitality Management* Part 4
Teare R. and Olsen M., *International Hospitality Management*
Witt S. F., Brooke M. Z. and Buckley P. J., *The Management of International Tourism*, Chapters 4, 7

# One Hundred Books for Students and Professionals

Abbott P. and Lewry S. (1991) *Front Office. Procedures, Social Skills and Management*, Butterworth-Heinemann, Oxford
Abbott P. and Shepherd J. (1989) *Hotel and Catering Case Studies*, Cassell, London
Allen D. (1983) *Accommodation and Cleaning Services*, Vols 1 & 2, Stanley Thornes, Cheltenham
Anderson C. and Blakemore D. (1991) *Modern Food Service*, Butterworth-Heinemann, Oxford
Andrioli S. and Douglas P. (1990) *Professional Food Service*, Butterworth-Heinemann, Oxford

Bareham J. and Beharrell B. (1987) *Cases in Hospitality Management*, Butterworth-Heinemann, Oxford
Boardman R. D. (1991) *Hotel and Catering Accounts*, Butterworth-Heinemann, Oxford
Boella M. J. (1992) *Human Resource Management in the Hospitality Industry*, Stanley Thornes, Cheltenham
Braham B. (1988) *Computer Systems in the Hotel and Catering Industry*, Cassell, London
Braham B. (1993) *Hotel Front Office*, Stanley Thornes, Cheltenham
Branson J. C. and Lennox M. (1988) *Hotel, Hostel and Hospital Housekeeping*, Hodder & Stoughton, Sevenoaks
Burkart A. J. and Medlik S. (1981) *Tourism – Past, Present and Future*, Butterworth-Heinemann, Oxford
Buttle F. (1986) *Hotel and Food Service Marketing. A Managerial Approach*, Cassell, London

Cooper C. P., ed. (1989, 1990, 1991) *Progress in Tourism, Recreation and Hospitality Management*, Vols 1, 2, 3, Belhaven Press, London
Cooper C. P. and Lockwood A., eds (1992, 1993) *Progress in Tourism, Recreation and Hospitality Management*, Vols 4, 5, Belhaven Press, London
Cunningham S. (1991) *Data Analysis in Hotel and Catering Management*, Butterworth-Heinemann, Oxford

Davis B. and Stone S. (1991) *Food and Beverage Management*, Butterworth-Heinemann, Oxford
Dix C. and Baird C. (1988) *Front Office Operations*, Pitman, London

Doswell R. (1970) *Towards an Integrated Approach to Hotel Planning*, New University Education, London

Fellows J. (1984) *Housekeeping Supervision*, Macdonald & Evans, London
Fellows R. and J. (1990) *Buildings for Hospitality. Principles of Care and Design for Accommodation Managers*, Pitman, London
Fenton L., Fowler N. A. and Parkinson G. S. (1989) *Hotel Accounts and Their Audit*, The Institute of Chartered Accountants in England and Wales, London
Fewell A. and Wills N. (1992) *Marketing. Hospitality Managers' Pocket Book Series*, Butterworth-Heinemann, Oxford
Fuller J. and Kirk D. (1991) *Kitchen Planning and Management*, Butterworth-Heinemann, Oxford
Fuller J. and Waller K. (1992) *The Menu, Food and Profit*, Stanley Thornes, Cheltenham

Gale K. (1985) *Behavioural and Supervisory Studies for Hotel and Catering Operations*, Stanley Thornes, Cheltenham
Gale K. and Odgers P. (1984) *Hotel and Catering Supervision*, Macdonald & Evans, London
Gamble P. (1984) *Small Computers and Hospitality Management*, Hutchinson, London
Gladwell D. C. (1981) *Practical Maintenance and Equipment*, Hutchinson, London
Godowski S. (1986) *Microcomputers in the Hotel and Catering Industry*, Butterworth-Heinemann, Oxford
Goss-Turner S. (1992) *Managing People in the Hotel and Catering Industry*, Croner, Kingston upon Thames
Greene M. (1987) *Marketing Hotels and Restaurants into the 90s*, Butterworth-Heinemann, Oxford
Gullen H. V. and Rhodes G. E. (1983) *Management in the Hotel and Catering Industry*, Batsford, London

Harris P. (1992) *Profit Planning. Hospitality Managers' Pocket Book Series*, Butterworth-Heinemann, Oxford
Harris P. and Hazzard P. (1987) *Accounting in the Hotel and Catering Industry*, Stanley Thornes, Cheltenham
Harris P. and Hazzard P. (1992) *Managerial Accounting in the Hotel and Catering Industry*, Stanley Thornes, Cheltenham
Hatfield D. and Winter C. (1986) *Professional Housekeeping*, Stanley Thornes, Cheltenham
Hodgson A. (1987) *The Travel and Tourism Industry. Strategies for the Future*, Pergamon, Oxford
Hornsey T. and Dann D. (1984) *Manpower Management in the Hotel and Catering Industry*, Batsford, London
Horwath Consulting in Europe (Annual) *European Hotel Industry*, Horwath Consulting, London
Horwath International (Annual) *Worldwide Hotel Industry* (formerly Worldwide Lodging Industry), HI, New York
Horwath & Horwath (UK) Ltd (1988) *Hotels of the Future. Strategies and Action Plan*. International Hotel Association, Paris
Hotel and Catering Training Board (1982) *Starting Up Your Own Business in the Hotel and Catering Industry*, HCTB, London
Hotel and Catering Training Board (1986) *Marketing for Hotels and Restaurants*, HCTB, London
Hotel and Catering Training Company (1989) *Accommodation Operations*, Macmillan/HCTC, London

Hotel and Catering Training Company (1990) *The Accommodation Operation*, HCTC, London

Hotel and Catering Training Company (1992) *Controlling Costs*, HCTC, London

Hotel and Catering Training Company (1991) *Employee Relations*, HCTC, London

Hotel and Catering Company (1990) *Front of House Operation*, Macmillan/HCTC, London

Hotel and Catering Training Company (1991) *Maximising Occupancy. How to Increase Rooms Sales*, HCTC, London

Housden J. (1984) *Franchising and Other Business Relationships in Hotel and Catering Services*, Butterworth-Heinemann, Oxford

Hughes H. L. (1989) *Economics for Hotel and Catering Students*, Stanley Thornes, Cheltenham

Hurst R. (1984) *Accommodation Management*, Heinemann, London

International Association of Hospitality Accountants (1986) *Uniform System of Accounts for Hotels*, 8th revised edition, Hotel Association of New York City Inc., New York

International Hotels Environment Initiative (1993) *Environmental Management for Hotels. The Industry Guide to Best Practice*, Butterworth-Heinemann, Oxford

Jones C. and Paul V. (1993) *Accommodation Management. A Systems Approach*, Batsford, London

Jones P. and Lockwood A. (1989) *The Management of Hotel Operations. An Innovative Approach to the Study of Hotel Management*, Cassell, London

Jones P. and Pizam A. eds (1993) *The International Hospitality Industry. Organisational and Operational Issues*, Pitman, London

Julyan B. (1991) *Beverage Sales and Service*, Butterworth-Heinemann, Oxford

Kinton R., Ceserani V. and Foskett D. (1992) *The Theory of Catering*, Hodder & Stoughton, Sevenoaks

Kotas R. (1981) *Accounting in the Hotel and Catering Industry*, Blackie, Glasgow

Kotas R. (1986) *Management Accounting for Hotels and Restaurants*, Blackie, Glasgow

Lennick J. (1989) *Running Your Own Small Hotel*, Kogan Page, London

Lennon J. and Peet M. (1990) *Hospitality Management: A Case Study Approach*, Hodder & Stoughton, Sevenoaks

Lillicrap D. R. and Cousins J. A. (1990) *Food and Beverage Service*, Hodder & Stoughton, Sevenoaks

Lockwood A. and Jones P. (1984) *People and the Hotel and Catering Industry. An Introduction to Behavioural Studies and Human Relations*, Cassell, London

Medlik, S. (1993) *Dictionary of Travel, Tourism and Hospitality*, Butterworth-Heinemann, Oxford

Medlik S., ed. (1991) *Managing Tourism*, Butterworth-Heinemann, Oxford

Medlik S. (1988) *Tourism and Productivity*, British Tourist Authority/English Tourist Board, London

Merricks P. and Jones P. (1986) *The Management of Catering Operations. An Innovative Approach to Food and Beverage Management*, Cassell, London

Messenger S. and Shaw H. (1993) *Financial Management for the Hospitality, Tourism and Leisure Industries*, Macmillan, Basingstoke

Messenger S. and Shaw H. (1991) *Hospitality Management Case Study Assignments*, Macmillan, Basingstoke

Middleton V. T. C. (1988) *Marketing in Travel and Tourism*, Butterworth-Heinemann, Oxford
Mullins L. (1992) *Hospitality Management. A Human Resources Approach*, Pitman, London

National Economic Development Committee (1992) *Costs and Manpower Productivity in UK Hotels*, National Economic Development Office, London

Odgers P. (1988) *The Hotel, Catering and Leisure Industry*, Stanley Thornes, Cheltenham
Odgers P. (1985) *Purchasing, Costing and Control for Hotel and Catering Operations*, Stanley Thornes, Cheltenham
Organisation for Economic Co-operation and Development (Annual) *Tourism Policy and International Tourism in OECD Member Countries*, OECD, Paris

Paige G. and J. (1984) *The Hotel Receptionist*, Cassell, London

Quest M., ed. (1990) *Horwath Book of Tourism*, Macmillan, London
Quest M. (1984) *How to Buy Your Own Hotel*, Hutchinson, London

Riley M. (1991) *Human Resource Management. A Guide to Personnel Practice in the Hotel and Catering Industries*, Butterworth-Heinemann, Oxford
Roberts J. (1993) *Marketing for the Hospitality Industry*, Hodder & Stoughton, Sevenoaks

Shepherd J. W. (1982) *Marketing Practice in the Hotel and Catering Industry*, Batsford, London
Smith J. (1990) *Practical Computing. A Guide for Hotel and Catering Students*, Butterworth-Heinemann, Oxford
Sutton D. F. (1983) *Financial Management in Hotel and Catering Operations*, Butterworth-Heinemann, Oxford

Taylor D. (1988) *Hotel and Catering Sales. A Complete Guide*, Butterworth-Heinemann, Oxford
Teare R. *et al.*, eds (1993) *Managing and Marketing Services into the 1990s*, Cassell, London
Teare R. *et al.*, eds (1992) *Managing Projects in Hospitality Organizations*, Cassell, London
Teare R. and Boer A., eds (1991) *Strategic Hospitality Management. Theory and Practice for the 1990s*, Cassell, London
Teare R. and Ingram H. (1993) *Strategic Management. A Resource-based Approach for the Hospitality and Tourism Industries*, Cassell, London
Teare R. and Olsen M. (1992) *International Hospitality Management. Corporate Strategy in Practice*, Pitman, London

Venison P. (1983) *Managing Hotels*, Butterworth-Heinemann, Oxford

Walton P. (1983) *Modern Financial Accounting in the Hospitality Industry*, Hutchinson, London
White P. B. and Beckley H. (1988) *Hotel Reception*, Hodder & Stoughton, Sevenoaks
Witt S. F., Brooke, M. Z. and Buckley P. J. (1991) *The Management of International Tourism*, Unwin Hyman, London
Witt S. F. and Moutinho L., eds (1989) *Tourism Marketing and Management Handbook*, Prentice Hall, Hemel Hempstead

Wood F. and Lightowlers P. (1983) *Accounting in the Hotel and Catering Industry*, Longman, Harlow

Wood F. and Lightowlers P. (1985) *Purchasing, Costing and Control in the Hotel and Catering Industry*, Longman, Harlow

Wood R. C. (1992) *Working in Hotels and Catering*, Routledge, London

World Tourism Organization (Annual) *Compendium of Tourism Statistics*, WTO, Madrid

# Index